Essentials of MadCap Mimic 6

Copyright Statement

This book was written by Neil Perlin, President of Hyper/Word Services (www.hyperword.com).

Please send all suggestions or corrections to nperlin@nperlin.cnc.net

Dedication

This book is dedicated to my wife Connie, whose courage allowed me to go on this ride. Couldn't have done it without you...

Table of Contents

Forward

"*Essentials of MadCap Mimic 6'* is a great reference for any user - new and experienced - of this powerful visual training development tool. The book introduces the concepts behind video training in order to give new users a solid foundation. The rest of the book then follows the steps of a typical and real-life project in order to explain the mechanics of Mimic usage, illustrating the steps with dozens of crucial, real-world design tips and ideas."

- Anthony Olivier, CEO, MadCap Software

1 Overview

Introduction

This book explains how to use MadCap Mimic to create screen "movies." You can use these movies to demonstrate features of your software or create simulations to let people "try" that software, but you can also use it to create role-playing training for use in sales, HR, and more.

You can provide these movies to users in stand-alone form. You can also integrate the movies into help systems created in MadCap Flare or other help authoring tools in order to create multi-modal help systems.

Audience

The book is for new Mimic authors, whether or not they've used similar tools. The book focuses on the mechanics of Mimic use but also covers the design, planning, and management aspects of creating movies. More specifically, the book covers:

- Mimic overview
- Movie planning and design
- Basic movie recording, "annotation", and output
- Advanced annotation and output
- Management and control features

Structure of This Book

Two notes about the structure of this book:

- You can read the book in any order, but it's written in a workflow-oriented sequence – create a basic movie, modify that movie to make it look the way you want, distribute it, and manage the movie-making process. So if you're new to Mimic, you can create a basic movie by reading chapters 2 – 8 in sequence. If you then want to go further and add interactive features, see chapter 9. To use special or advanced features, see chapter 10.

- Mimic uses the same or similar dialog box tabs in many places, which makes it easy to learn and use. Because of that repetition, the book only shows a screen shot of each tab once, the first time that the book refers to it.

2 Mimic Overview

What Is Mimic?

Have you ever taught a co-worker to perform some task in a program by doing the steps as the co-worker watches? And done it again for other co-workers? What if you could perform the steps once, record them, add explanations, and make the result available to everyone? That's what Mimic can do.

As you perform the task, Mimic automatically records each step as a separate screen shot. When you finish, you can add textual explanations or visual elements like highlights for emphasis in order to make the screen shots more helpful. You can then output the series of screen shots as a filmstrip – effectively a "movie" – for users to run.

Why create such movies? A few examples…

- Tech support hears the same questions over and over. If you can identify the top twenty questions, you can create movies to answer each one and post them on a "help" page on your company intranet. This might let tech support focus on more unusual or advanced questions.

- Marketing can create movies that demo the company's products and make the movies available to prospective clients on the company's web site.

- Training might create movies that introduce users to the basics of the company's products. Trainers can then deal with specific or advanced questions rather than having to explain everything from scratch over and over. As a side benefit, travel expenses might decline.

- The disaster recovery team might create movies that show how to get the servers up and running for reference by junior staff in the backup facility.

Mimic's Interface

The default interface has seven main sections: Left pane, Editing pane, Right pane, Bottom pane, Menus, Global toolbars, and Local toolbars.

We'll first discuss the basic interface. Later in this chapter, you'll see how to customize the interface.

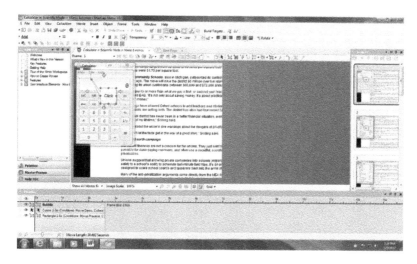

Left Pane

By default, the Movies and Palettes tabs open in the left pane. You'll see the tab labels in an accordion structure at the bottom of the left pane, as shown below.

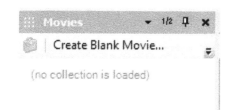

Movies Tab

The Movies tab shows a thumbnail of the first frame of each movie in a multi-movie *collection* (as opposed to individual movies). If you're creating an *individual movie*, this window indicates (no collection is loaded).

Note – When you click a tab in the accordion list at the bottom of the screen, Mimic highlights it in orange (grey on some PCs).

Palettes Tab

The Palettes tab lets you save slide objects like text callouts in a "library" for re-use.

If you use MadCap Flare, you'll find that Mimic's palettes are conceptually similar to Flare's snippets.

The accordion structure shows four tab labels. Additional tabs appear as icons at the bottom of the accordion list, as shown below. Here, the fifth tab – the key icon – is the Help index tab. Clicking on it opens that tab.

The following windows also appear in the Left Pane by default:

Window Name	Description
Master Frames	List master frames (used to insert common objects like buttons, on multiple frames in a movie).
Help TOC	Display the help's table of contents.

Help Browse Sequence	Browse sequentially through topics in the help.
Help Index	Display the help's index.
Help Search	Search for information in the help.
Help Favorites	Display a list of help topics that you marked as favorites for easy retrieval over and over again.
Help Glossary	Display help terms and their definitions.

To close a window, click the X icon on its title bar. To open a window, select **View** and the window.

Frame Pane

The Frame pane displays in the middle of the interface. You'll use it to edit each frame in a movie or display the Link Browser if you need a flowchart view of the frames. You can close panes on the left or right sides of the Frame pane to get extra working room, as shown below.

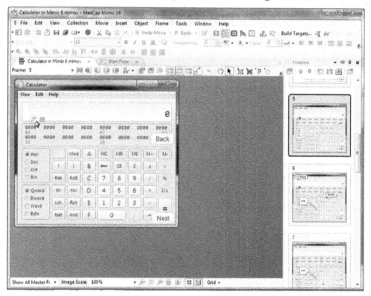

You can have multiple windows open in the Frame pane, each indicated by a tab at the top of the pane. In the example above, there are two, for a movie called Calculator in Mimic 6.mimov and for the Start Page.

Start Page

The Start Page offers quick access to information and main tasks. You can open an existing project or collection, create a new one, access the online help and startup documentation, visit the Mimic Help Community, and get news from MadCap.

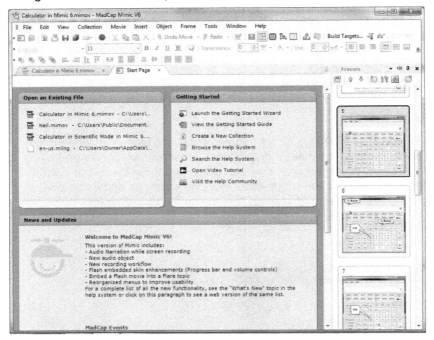

To display the Start Page, select **View > Start Page** or click the Open the Start Page icon ⬚ on the main toolbar.

Mimic's Online Help

Mimic has an extensive online help system. By default, the help table of contents, index, search, glossary, and favorites windows display in the left pane. The help topics themselves appear in the Frame pane.

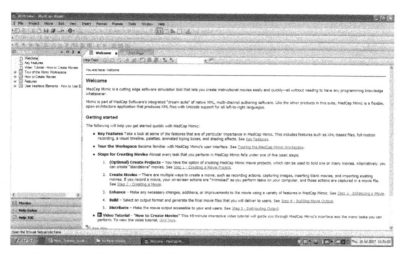

To display the help, select Help and the desired submenu item.

Frame Editor

The Frame editor lets you create and edit individual frames in a movie.

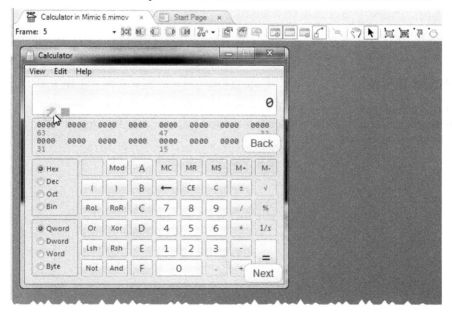

Mimic's Resemblance to MadCap Flare

If you own Flare, notice how its interface resembles Mimic's. Below, for example, is Flare's XML Editor where you write or edit topics. The interface similarities reduce the learning curve across different MadCap tools.

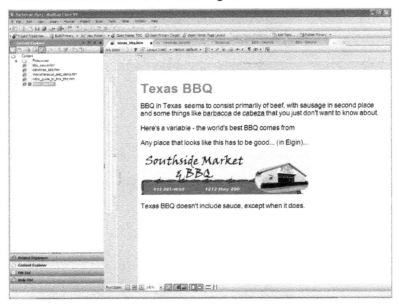

Right Pane

The Frames window opens by default in the right pane. It lists all frames in the movie and lets you navigate between frames, add frames, or resequence frames.

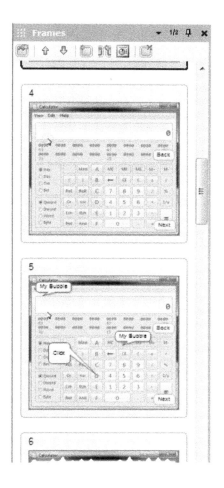

To go to a specific frame, single-click on it in the frame list.

Bottom Pane

The Timeline, Messages, and Status windows open in the bottom pane.

- Timeline – Controls the timing of frames and objects on frames.

- Messages – Lists the results of an index search, error messages, and the timeline.

- Status – Shows information like the coordinates of the upper left corner of an object.

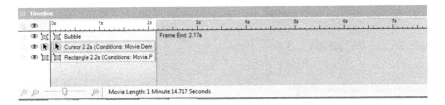

Menus

The menus offer all of Mimic's functionality.

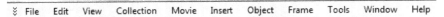

Many menu commands also have toolbar icons and/or shortcut keys. If they do, the icons and keys are listed on the menu.

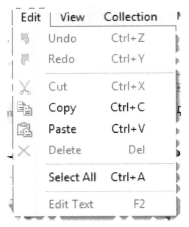

An icon to the left of a menu item *usually* means the item is on a toolbar. If a menu item has a keyboard shortcut, it's listed to the right of the item.

Toolbars

When you start Mimic for the first time, you'll see the Standard toolbar.

Standard Toolbar

The Standard toolbar let you do basic tasks like save, cut, and copy, and offers various shortcut buttons for movie work. To see this toolbar, part of which is shown below, select **View** > **Toolbars** > **Standard**.

Other Toolbars

You can also show or hide these toolbars:

- Format – To control text formatting and effects like shadowing.

- Frames – To add, delete, or move frames, or record new frames.

- Layout – To control the alignment and sequence of objects on a frame.

To show one of these toolbars, select **View > Toolbars** and the toolbar.

Customizing the Interface

The interface is almost fully customizable. You can adjust each window's setting by using the icons in that window's title bar.

Moving windows

To move a window, click the Drag Pane icon ⠿ on the window title bar and drag, or click the down arrow in the window title bar and select **Floating**. In the screen shown below, the Help TOC pane is floating.

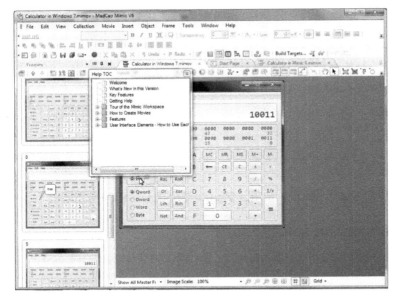

Tip – If you have two monitors, you can move some windows to the second monitor and devote the other to the frame editing.

Docking a floating window

"Docking" a window means attaching it to a fixed location on the screen. To do so, click in the window's title bar and drag it to the area where you want to dock it so that the mouse pointer is on top of one of the blue docking arrows, shown below. Placing the pointer on the center target docks the window in the center of the window where the target appears. Experiment with the docking arrows to see which is the most useful.

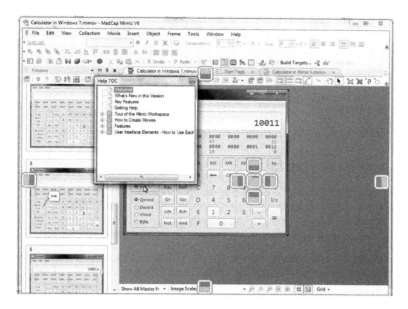

Auto-hiding window panes

At the right side of each window title bar is an ⛏ icon. Clicking it "pins" the window to the edge of the screen, "hiding" it and displaying only the window title on a tab on the edge of the screen, shown below. Hovering the mouse over the tab displays the window until you move the mouse off the tab. Click the push pin again to "un-pin" the window.

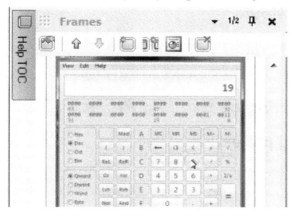

Widening a window

To temporarily make a window half-screen width, click the ¹ᐟ² icon on its title bar. Click the icon again to restore the window to its original width.

Closing a window

To close a window, click the standard Windows X icon on its title bar.

Working with layouts

A layout is a specific group of toolbars and windows. Mimic automatically saves changes to your window layouts using the **Window > Layouts > Auto-save Window Layout** option, so it always opens in the same toolbar/window configuration that it had when you closed it).

Tip – You can create and save different layouts for different tasks, like optimizing one layout as you need for adding text captions and another for inserting images. To do so, modify the interface, select **Windows > Layouts > Save Window Layout As...** and give it a name that defines the task, such as "Text caption layout". To load a saved layout, select **Window > Layouts** and pick the desired layout from the list.

Tip – If you changed the interface, don't like the result, and want to undo the changes, you can modify the interface backwards or just reset to the factory default, which may be faster and easier. To do the latter, select **Window > Layouts > Reset Window Layout** and accept the warning.

Closing an Open Movie

To close an open movie:

1. Select **File > Close** OR Click the x icon on the movie's tab.

Opening and Running an Existing Project

To open an existing project:

1. Select **File > Open**.

   The Open dialog box opens.

2. Locate and select the project.

3. Click **Open**.

You'll see the frames listed in the Frames pane, and the first frame opens in the Frame editing pane.

Alternatively:

1. Select **File > Recent Files**.

2. Locate and select the desired project.

Managing the List of Recent Projects

The more you work, the more entries you'll see in the Open an Existing Files list on the start page. This list shows all recent projects, including those you no longer want and even those you've deleted. So you'll want to clean up this list periodically.

To clean up the list of recent files.

1. Select **File > Recent Files > Manage Recent Files**. A Recent Files dialog box opens. Entries in red were deleted from your PC but are still in the list.

2. Click on the file(s) to be removed, then click the Remove button.

3 Movie Planning and Design

It's crucial to plan movies in general, and because of how Mimic works. Mimic can automatically record tasks you perform in an application. This automatic recording lets you devote your attention to the application rather than splitting your attention between the application and Mimic. It's a very efficient way to work.

However, Mimic records *everything* you do. If you realize half-way into recording a task that you forgot to set an option in the application, just set the option… but Mimic records your setting the option. No problem; just delete the extra frames from the movie. But why not do it right the first time? By planning.

"Planning" implies planning the steps in a movie but also means defining the goals and audience, designing according to those definitions, developing, and so on. Most planning methodologies are too detailed for Mimic work. In the time you spent planning, you could finish the movie. But there is a methodology called ADDIE that's well suited to Mimic. ADDIE stands for:

- A – Analyze.
- D – Design.
- D – Develop.
- I – Implement.
- E – Evaluate.

Two important points about ADDIE.

- You probably won't be able to do everything discussed in this chapter, but the more you can the better.
- ADDIE is circular. When you reach the Evaluate step, it's time to return to the Analyze step to assess the results and modify the movie as needed. This is hard because we assume that once we finish a movie and send it out to the field, it's done. But, in theory, this circularity means a movie is never done; you should always be soliciting feedback, evaluating it, and modifying the movie as need be. This may take a cultural shift in your group.

We'll now review the ADDIE steps. Remember that this chapter can't account for the peculiarities of your situation. Take the discussion as a guide to adapt to your own needs.

Analyze

In this phase, you're defining the environment for your movies. Consider:

Goals – What Do You Want To Accomplish?

What are the goals? For example, to create movies that show features of your company's software or show its ease of use? Different goals may require different tone and flow.

In defining the goals, you have to answer two questions:

- What *must* viewers learn?
- What would be *nice* for viewers to learn?

Tip – If you're creating movies to help viewers use your company's software, you can learn a lot about what to show in the movies by talking to the people in the tech support and training groups.

Depending If you're having trouble defining a movie, you may have too many goals. Consider breaking it into separate, linked movies.

How do you define the goals? Partly on what you know about the needs of the company, and partly by talking to related groups, like tech support.

Audience(s) – Who Are the Viewers

You should know several things about your viewers.

- Do they know how to use PCs? New users may not know what a browser is or what "cut-and-paste" means.

- Do they know how to work online? We think they know what it means when the mouse pointer turns into a pointing finger but novice viewers, who most need our movies, may not. Might you need to create a movie that explains how to use Mimic movies?

- Do they have the "domain knowledge" to understand the movie? For example, in a movie about picking a fixed asset depreciation method in accounting software, will viewers know the difference between the choices or must you explain them?

- Can you take steps for granted? If a movie shows how to log in to a server, must it show how to get to the login screen?

- Are the viewers proficient in English? It's always good to write simply, but crucial if the viewers are not. This may lead you to pause a movie after each frame and add a "Click to continue" button to let viewers read and advance at their own pace.

Tip – You can learn a lot about your viewers by, again, talking to the people in the tech support and training groups.

Resources and Constraints – Some Questions

Do you have enough time and money for the work? Do you have time to do the work with in-house staff or do you need to bring in contractors? Are local contractors available or do you need to get remote contractors? Does this fit company policy or will you need a waiver?

Consider your information sources. Can you get to SMEs (subject matter experts), programmers, etc? Can you schedule time with them? Can you talk to customers to discuss issues like training needs or documentation?

Are there any other constraints?

Distribution

How will you distribute movies to reviewers during development and viewers at the end? Do the recipients have web access and the required browsers? Can you send movies through your or your viewers' firewalls?

Notes about This Phase

There's a lot to look at in this phase, but you may already know most of it. Unless you're new to your company, or new to Mimic and this type of authoring, this phase shouldn't take more than a few days.

Design

In this phase, you're designing and testing the movie prototype based on the results of the analysis phase. Consider:

Plan the Mimic Feature Set

Decide which Mimic features to use. Ideally, define a standard feature set for all movies in order to present a consistent face to viewers. To do so, you have to learn what features Mimic offers and coordinate with other Mimic authors.

This book describes most of Mimic's major features. You'll learn more on your own as you use Mimic. Also learn what other groups that use Mimic are doing in order to decide if *all groups* should present a consistent face to viewers or whether to make movies from different groups deliberately look different.

Create a Visual Style Guide

Once you pick the features to use, try to create a style guide that defines their settings. You can create standard text callouts, highlight boxes, and similar features and save them in palettes for re-use in other movies. You can also send palettes to other developers to ensure consistency.

Create an Outline of the Movie

Why create an outline? Three reasons:

- Mimic captures everything you do; an outline reduces the risk of doing the wrong things.

- There are steps you perform that you don't think about until you have to tell someone what to do. Creating an outline makes you think about those steps.

- Recording a basic movie just creates a bunch of frames showing what's on the screen at each step. Before your movie is finished, you'll probably want to modify the text callouts Mimic added, add highlight boxes and other objects, add a title slide, and more. The outline will help you plan and control these added features.

The outline can be a screen-by-screen list of each step in the task you're recording. It can be graphic or simple text descriptions of each screen.

After creating an outline, do dry runs to be sure you didn't miss a step. Modify the outline after each dry run and try again until it's okay. The result is a shooting script to guide your work.

Storyboarding – Formalizing the Outline

An outline helps you clarify what you're doing and find potential errors, but its usefulness is often limited because it's rough. You can make it more useful by turning it into a storyboard, a formalized outline that can serve three purposes.

- It adds detail. In addition to a sketch or description of a screen, a storyboard can include instructions on what to do to get to the next screen, objects (callouts, etc.) to add to the frame, etc. It's a capsule summary of the work for development purposes.

- It's archivable for use by the next author.

- It helps "sell" a movie. Many clients can't picture how a movie will flow. But you can tape each storyboard sheet to a conference room wall and walk the client through the movie, frame by frame.

An easy way to create a storyboard is to draw or describe each frame, ideally one frame per page to give yourself room. Then add details about the frame's timing, the screen objects it contains, the timing relationships between them, and so on. This approach is simple and quick but rough.

Develop a Writing Style Guide

To get consistency between different movies and developers, create a writing style guide. Don't get too nit-picky; focus on issues that are open to question or specific to writing for Mimic.

Create a Prototype

After collecting or defining this information, test it by using it to create a movie prototype. The prototype should cover a real topic and have as many features as possible that would appear in a typical movie that you'll be creating, so that the usability testing will be as comprehensive as possible. The movie should also be short, so that you won't spend too much time on it.

Conduct a Usability Test

QA looks at whether links work, for example; usability looks at whether users can find the desired link at all. Many companies don't test usability, but a movie is a waste of time and effort if viewers can't use it.

You can test usability in dedicated labs, but they're expensive. Instead, you can do ad hoc testing. Some suggestions:

- Test early in order to have time to fix problems before release. If you test near the end of a project, you may find problems but not have time to fix them. You'll have to fix them in the next release, annoying the users until then.

- Use a range of testers who replicate real viewers. If you can, run the tests at user group meetings where there's a big pool of test subjects. If that's not possible, invite nearby users in or just grab people at random out of the hall. None of these approaches give statistically valid data, but they will produce a lot of *good* data.

- Keep tests short, under an hour, and give testers a thank-you gift – ideally something unusual that they'll display prominently on an office shelf. Enter testers in a drawing for dinner at a restaurant as a further prize. The idea is to make participation fun in order to turn testers into evangelists for your next usability test.

- Don't sit testers in front of a PC, run the movie, and ask what they think. Instead, build scenarios with questions whose answers are in the movie. For example, tell your testers that the movie will show how to log into your application and that, at the end, you'll ask how many characters they need for a password. In other words, make the questions concrete.

- Sit and watch quietly as testers go through the movie. Time them. Do not give hints if they have trouble. You want to see if they have problems and, if so, if they can find their way out.

Review and Use the Test Results

Review the test results for problems in the movie's flow or interface and modify the prototype. Then retest to see if you fixed the problems.

Notes about This Phase

There's a lot to do in this phase, but style definition is quick and its benefits often apply across multiple movies. Prototyping is also quick, as you'll see in the next module. Finally, usability testing and evaluation is also quick, often no more than a day to run a test and assess the results.

Develop

In this phase, you're creating the actual movie(s), based on the results of the prototyping. Consider:

Record the Screens

There are two ways to grab screens, auto-capture (default) and manual. Manual provides the most control; you record exactly what you want. However, auto-capture handles the details of recording for you, letting you focus on the content of your movie rather than the mechanics of creating it. Because of that, you may find auto-capture the most effective method.

Recording is simple. All you're really doing is running the application and letting Mimic record the screens. Your work begins in the next step – frame annotation.

Annotate the Frames

After recording the frames, make them more useful by adding things like:

- Callout boxes that provide explanations and instructions.

- Highlight boxes or arrows that draw attention to areas of a frame.

- Rollovers that pop up a graphic or text when viewers move the mouse over an area of the screen.

- Graphics – screen shots, photos, company logos, etc.

- Audio like voice narration for a frame, linked buttons, click boxes that simulate menu selections for interaction simulations, etc.

Annotation is the most time-consuming part of the work.

Preview and Modify

Preview often – each time you add a slide, alter the timing of a callout on a slide, and so on. You can preview:

- The entire movie.

- The current frame.

- From the current frame to the end of the movie.

- The current frame plus 5 or 10 slides.

Tip – Previewing the entire movie on a regular basis is a waste of time if you just want to check a few slides. The 5 or 10 frame options may be the most useful.

Be sure to have users preview the movie too. They'll see things that are clear to you, because of your familiarity with the movie, but not to them.

Generate the Finished Output for Distribution

When you finish development, generate and publish a finished version for users.

Notes about This Phase

This is where you apply everything from the first two phases.

Implement

In this phase, you make the finished movie available. It's straightforward since all you're doing is distributing the files that form the finished movies and, if possible, providing a feedback mechanism. The main issues have to do with the distribution methods, not the actual movies. Consider:

Distribute the Movies

This may be through a combination of:

- Loading them on a web site for viewers to watch from the site or download and watch locally.

- Burning them onto DVDs or other device for distribution to viewers who can watch the movies locally.

Provide Feedback Mechanisms

Authors often lose track of a movie after distribution. Is anyone watching it? Are there errors or problems? Often, we don't know. Some authors send hard-copy evaluation forms but the response rate is usually poor. It's inconvenient to fill out and mail a form, and people rarely do it.

If the viewers have network access, feedback is simpler. You might add a feedback button that jumps viewers to a feedback form on your company's web site. Viewers can fill out and send the form with a few mouse clicks. If you have the budget, send a gift to viewers who give feedback, as in the usability tests. Feedback rates will never be high but they'll go up and that's what you want – more and better feedback from viewers whose view of feedback has gone from negative to positive.

Evaluate

In this phase, you evaluate the feedback and modify the output. This task often gets short shrift due to (seemingly) more pressing demands of new projects but it's in this phase that your culture becomes one of continual improvement. Consider:

Analyze/Review the Feedback

Categorize the feedback. Ideally, it falls into a few categories:

- Technical errors.
- Unclear writing.

- Formatting problems.
- Other problems.

If you link to feedback forms, consider basing them on these categories.

After reviewing the feedback, prioritize it and modify the movie. You *must* fix technical errors. Fix unclear writing if it can cause errors. You *should* fix format or similar problems, but they'll have a lower priority unless they hurt accuracy or usability.

Workflow Review

This chapter ends with a review of the overall workflow and some tasks that fall outside ADDIE.

- Determine the users' screen resolutions.

  You must know the screen size on which movies will run. Too big a movie won't fit on older monitors. For example, if you create movies to fit your 1280x1024 monitor, those movies add vertical and horizontal scroll bars when run on 800x600 monitors. The solution is to determine what monitors your viewers have before you start creating movies and develop for the smallest size. You *can* resize a movie if you picked the wrong size, but that makes extra work for you.

- Ask the programmers what graphics cards they support since different colors may display differently on different graphic cards.
- Set standards, including a standard size for movie screens, plus a style guide, objects etc. Consider creating a movie template.
- Prepare your PC if you intend to shoot smaller than full-screen. Hide desktop wallpaper, turn off color gradients, and move icons out of the screen capture area.
- Create the storyboard, plus a script if you plan to add voiceovers.
- Set any desired general Mimic options, like what panes to display where, what spelling dictionary to use, etc.
- Set any desired specific movie options.
- Record the movie.
- Add captions and other screen annotations and effects.
- Preview often and adjust as needed.

- Generate the final output.
- Distribute.
- Solicit feedback from *real* users.

4 Recording Movies

Creating Basic Movies

A basic movie is just a set of frames. If you're recording software, each frame shows a screen on which you did something, like clicking a menu item, or a screen that you captured manually. It's a fast way to create movies; if you use Mimic's default settings, it does most of the work in the background, automatically recording the screen as you concentrate on the application itself.

The book focuses on this kind of movie. But when the book discusses screen annotation features, you'll see how you can also use Mimic to create non-software movies, like role-playing simulations.

After you capture all the screens that form the basic movie, you'll add more content, explanations, visual cues, and other objects on the frames to make them more useful. All these Mimic features are easy to use mechanically. The crucial thing is using them well together. As you create movies, remember that you're competing against multimedia, the web, "real" movies, and other elements of our visual society.

Movies vs. Collections

Mimic lets you create two kinds of projects. A "movie" is a set of files and settings that form one specific movie. A "collection" is two or more linked but separate movies. You don't have to create a collection to create linked movies. You *can* create and link separate movies. But creating a collection has some useful benefits. Most of the book focuses on movies. "Collections" are covered in the last chapter.

Note – To avoid confusion, I'll use the term "movie" to refer specifically to a movie, the term "collection" to refer specifically to a collection, and the term "project" when referring generically to movies or collections.

How Many Movies Do You Need?

Consider two issues when deciding how many movies to create:

- The number of specific tasks to teach or present. This is an instructional design issue. Each movie should cover one task.

- The duration of each movie you need. There's no "official" length but they should be short, if only to keep viewers' attention. You can always create and link several short movies. For example…

Imagine that a co-worker asks you to explain how to do a task in WordPad. You demonstrate the task to your co-worker and ask "Are you ready to try?" Your co-worker says "No. Show me once more." So you do, and again ask "Are you ready to try?" Your co-worker says "Yes." You give the co-worker the mouse and say "Okay, go." Now take this analogy to Mimic.

You create two movies. The first shows how to perform the task, and the viewer watches. The last frame asks "Are you ready to try?" and has Yes and No buttons. Clicking No re-runs the movie from the start; Yes jumps to a simulation which the viewer has to "run" as if it's the real thing. The "Yes" button is linked from the first movie to the second. The result is "branching", the ability to take viewers on different paths through different movies depending on how they interact with those movies.

Backing Up

To back up a Mimic movie, copy its .mimovf folder. For example, to back up a movie called Calculator in Windows 7, copy the folder Calculator in Windows 7.mimovf, shown below.

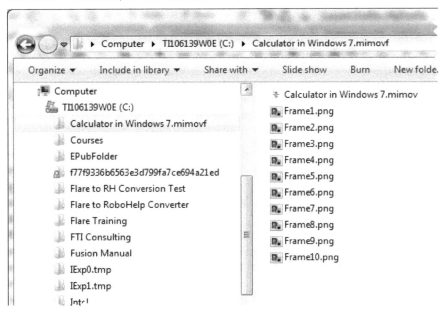

To backup a collection, copy everything in and below the project folder. For example, to backup a collection called Word Features that contains two movies called Search and Styles, copy the Word Features folder, the Styles.mimovf and Search.mimovf folders, and all folders and files below.

Recording Screens to Create a Raw Movie

A "raw" movie simply contains screen shots. It's simple to create:

- Start Mimic.
- Start and configure the application to the point that you want to start recording, including loading any file to use to demonstrate the task.
- Start a new movie project in Mimic.
- Configure Mimic's recording settings as necessary.
- Start using the application and record the screens.
- Stop recording when you've gotten the screens you need.

To record a raw movie as a demonstration:

1. Start Mimic.
2. Start the application that you want to record and configure it as necessary.
3. Switch back to Mimic.
4. Select **File > New** and the desired option from the New screen.

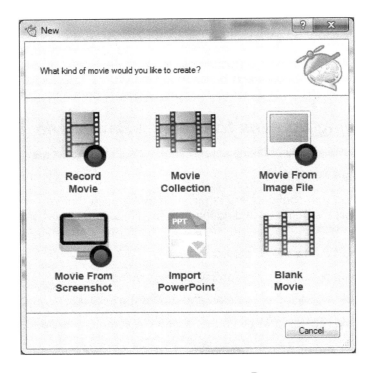

OR click the Record New Movie icon  on the toolbar. In either case, the recording screen displays.

You can now set the recording size and options, and enable or disable the mike depending on whether you want to record the narration as you create the movie.

- Recording size – Select one of the predefined sizes or:

  - *Snap to Window* to snap the red recording box to fit around the application window that you're recording.

If you select this option, the Select Window dialog box lists all running applications. Click the one to record.

- *Move Window into Rectangle* to fit the application into the red recording box whose size you set using one of the predefined sizes or set manually in the width and height fields.

  If setting the size manually, you can click the aspect ratio icon, between the Width and Height fields, to keep or turn off the automatic height-to-width adjustment.

  Tip – If one or more developers are creating multiple movies that viewers may watch sequentially, the Move Window into Rectangle option lets you force all the movies to one consistent size. For example, you might decide to use a 790 x 545 window for all the movies. Each developer would set this size and click the Move Window into Rectangle option to get a consistent movie window size no matter the different sizes of each developer's application window.

- Recording Options – Click the Options icon to display the Recording Options dialog box.

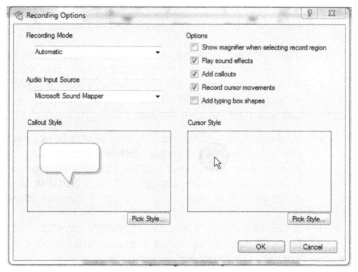

The Recording Options dialog box offers these options:

- Recording Mode – Automatic automatically captures every screen on which you perform an action. (Screens on which you don't perform an action aren't captured. To capture them, press the PrintScreen/PrtSc key.) Manual captures screens only when you press the PrintScreen/PrtSc key. (This lets you capture exactly what you want but splits your concentration between running the application and running Mimic). Video captures the entire movie as full motion video in one frame. (This is useful if you want to record real video but complicates the use of sequential callouts and similar features because you have to fit them into a single frame.)

- Audio Input Source – Select the desired source if you want to record narration simultaneously as you record the movie.

  Tip – Recording a movie and its narration together seems to make sense but can be surprisingly difficult. You're trying to simultaneously do two things that each demands a lot of concentration. You may find it easier to instead record the movie first and add the audio in a separate step.

- Show magnifier when selecting record region – Applies a magnifying glass effect when you select a region to record. Use this feature if you need to precisely select the recording region boundary.

- Play sound effects – Generates a click sound every time you capture a screen while recording.

  Tip – Always use this option to get confirmation that you captured a particular screen. Otherwise, you may not be sure that you captured a screen and may wind up capturing it twice, then have to delete the extra frame later. Viewers will not hear the click sound.

- Add callouts – Automatically add text callout boxes as you perform Windows-standard actions like clicking menu items. For each action, Mimic adds a callout with the word "Click" that points to where you clicked. You can edit or delete the callouts or add new ones after you finish recording.

  If you select the Add callouts option, the Callout Style button lets you select from a set of pre-defined callout styles. You can always change their attributes later.

- Record cursor... – Records the mouse pointer movement as you create the movie and plays it as the movie runs. Some authors use this option because mouse motion attracts the eye and makes the movie look real. Others find it distracting and hide the pointer in favor of using callouts and highlights.

  If you select the Record cursor movement option, click the Cursor Style button to select from a set of pre-defined styles. You can always change their attributes later.

- Add typing box shapes – Select to automatically add a typing box if you type text while recording in Automatic mode. De-selecting this option turns the frame on which you type text into a full-motion video frame. However, you won't be able to add other annotation objects, like text callouts, to the frame.

5. Click the Record option in the recording controls pane. Mimic gives a 3-2-1 countdown; you're then recording.

   The recording controls pane displays at the bottom of the recording area. You can select:

   - Shift icon or Shift/Pause keys – Pause recording. (The Pause key is near the PrtSc or PrintScreen key.)
   - Finish icon or End or Pause key – Start/Stop recording.

6. Perform the steps for the task that you want to record.

7. When you finish, press the End key to stop recording.

   You return to Mimic, which now shows the frames that form your raw movie.

Saving Your Work

Save often.

To save:

1. Select **File** > and the desired option.

   - **Save** – Saves any changes in the active file.

   - **Save As** – Saves the active file under a new name, in a different location, or as a different file type and automatically open the saved file in the Mimic editor.

   - **Save All** – Saves all changes in all open files, active or not.

Previewing a Movie

Preview a new movie immediately to be sure it's what you want before you start annotating it. Otherwise, you may do a lot of work on a movie that isn't what you wanted. And preview often during annotation work.

There are five preview options:

- **Movie** – Previews the entire movie. Use this after recording to be sure the movie is what you want, and before publishing the final output. To preview a frame or a frame transition, use one of the other options.

- **This Frame** – Previews the current frame.

- **Start at This Frame** – Previews from the current frame to the end.

- **Next 5 Frames** – Previews the current frame and the next four.

- **Next 10 Frames** – Previews the current frame and the next nine.

Each options displays in the MadCap Movie Player window.

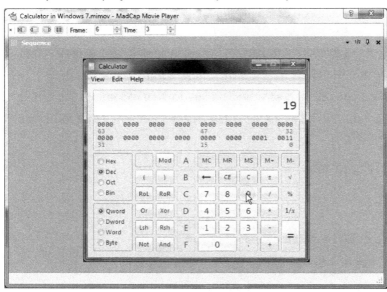

The MadCap Movie Player toolbar, shown below, lets you play or backup if you're previewing a movie, and adds the option to advance or backup to a different section if you're previewing a collection.

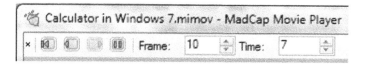

1. Select **Movie > Quick-Preview Movie** and the desired option

   OR click the Quick-Preview Movie icon [icon] dropdown and select **Movie**.

   The MadCap Movie Player window opens. Preview the movie using the player controls.

Closing a Movie or Collection

You can have multiple movies or collections open at one time, but your PC may bog down if they're too large or your PC has low memory.

To close a movie or collection:

1. Select **File > Close** OR **File > Close Collection**.

   You can now create or open another project, or select **File > Exit** to exit Mimic.

Closing All Open Movies or Collections

If you have too many movies or collection open, your PC may bog down or get cluttered. You can close movies or collections in two ways – the **Close All Documents** command or the **Close All Documents Except This One** command, which closes all movies or collections except the one you're looking at.

To close all open windows:

1. Select **Window > Close All Documents** OR **Window > Close All Documents Except This One**.

   Mimic will prompt you to save any unsaved movies or collections before closing them.

Opening a Movie or Collection

If you don't change the location, Mimic stores new movies or collections in the **My Documents\My Mimic Movies** folder.

To open a movie or collection:

1. Select **File > Open**. (If you previously opened the project, you can select **File > Recent Files or Recent Collections**.

    The Open dialog box appears.

2. Locate and select the movie or collection. (Movie files have a .mimovf extension, collection files have a .miprj extension.)

3. Click **Open**.

    The project opens in Mimic.

5 Basic Frame Annotation

About Frame Annotation

Frame annotation consists of adding features to frames to make them more helpful or add explanation. For example, you might:

- Add a frame to a movie to serve as its title page.

- Add a frame with a callout to introduce the movie – "In this movie, you'll see how to change a font…"

- Modify the callouts that Mimic automatically inserted or add new ones.

- Add highlight boxes that draw the viewer's eye to an area.

Most annotation features are straightforward by themselves. A callout is just a box with text in it, for example. The complexity comes from three other factors.

- There are many annotation features. Use a subset so as not to visually saturate viewers.

- Each annotation feature has many options. Again, use a subset so as not to visually saturate viewers.

- You may have to create content for some features. For example, a callout is just a box with text, but you have to write that text accurately and clearly.

Mimic uses a different approach toward such features than similar tools. It ships with fewer pre-defined annotation objects like callouts, but offers a huge number of customization options for such features.

Only use the annotation features that support a movie's goals. Don't use features because they're cool; they'll just distract the viewers. Keep your movies focused and simple.

This chapter introduces the basic annotation features that you'd use in a simple demo-style movie.

Callouts

Callouts are conceptually identical to speech bubbles in a comic strip – text in a box that refers to something.

Callouts are a widely used annotation feature, typically for three reasons.

- General description – To describe a movie or frame in general, like the example below. This callout has no pointer arrow since it's not referring to anything specific on the screen. You can set "no-arrow" as an attribute for a callout.

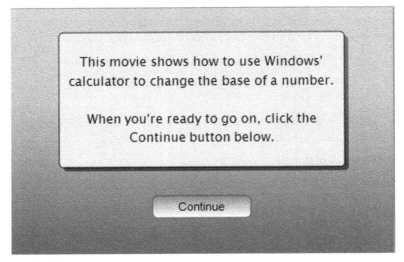

- Specific description – To refer to specific items in a frame like the base conversion options in the example below. This sample has an arrow because it's pointing to something on the screen.

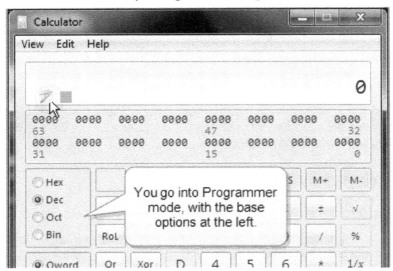

- Instructional – To actually give instructions. The callout below tells viewers to click a menu item and points out that item.

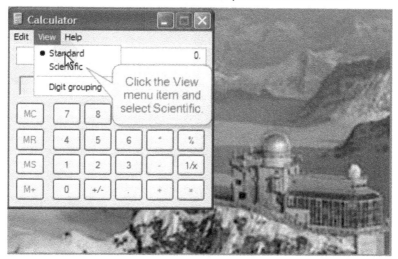

Creating Callouts

1. Display the frame on which you want to add the callout.

   You can use the Frames pane, or type the number in the Frame field at the left side of the Frame pane toolbar.

2. Click the Bubble Mode icon on the Frame Editor toolbar.

   The pointer changes to a small cross-hair.

   Tip – Depending on what you call a "callout," you can pick the Text Rectangle Mode icon or the Rectangle, Oval, or Polygon Mode options to create "shapes containing text." The difference is that the modes don't have a pointer option like Bubble mode.

3. Click roughly where the callout will go, hold the left mouse button down, and drag out a rectangle. You can adjust the size or position at any time.

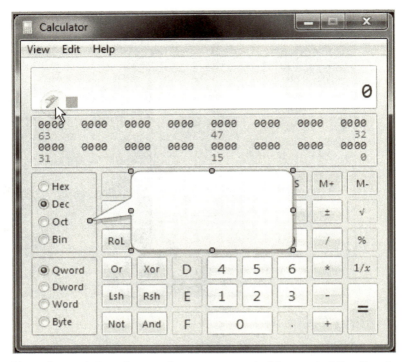

Note the grab handles on the corners and sides and at the tip of the arrow.

Click on and drag any of the grab handles to resize. Click in the callout and drag to move the box and pointer arrow. Click on the little bubble icon in the lower right corner of the callout and drag to move the callout box but leave the tip of the pointer arrow fixed.

To add text in a callout without opening the full properties dialog box, click on the callout to select it and start typing. A text insertion box immediately opens on top of the callout. Type the text, and use the options at the top of the insertion box to format text or add a variable. When you finish, click outside the insertion box to close it.

4.   To set the callout's properties, double click on the box. The Bubble Properties dialog box opens.

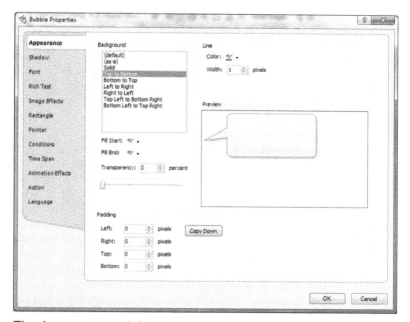

The Appearance tab lets you set the callout box's basic color and border values:

- **Background** — To set the background color as solid or a color gradient, such as green shading to yellow, in different directions.

- **Fill Start/Fill End** — To set the starting and ending colors if you set a gradient for the background.

- **Transparency** — To set the degree of transparency of the background colors.

- **Padding** – To set the amount of blank space between the edges of the callout box and the text.

- **Copy Down button** – To re-use your entry in the first Padding field in the remaining three padding fields.

- **Color** – To set the color of the callout box's border.

- **Width** – To set the width of the callout box's border.

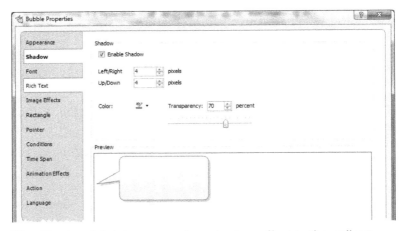

The Shadow tab lets you apply a shadow effect to the callout box:

- **Enable Shadow** — To turn on the shadow effect.

- **Left/Right** — To set the shadow's horizontal offset from the callout box.

- **Up/Down** — To set the shadow's vertical offset from the callout box.

- **Color** – To set the shadow's color.

- **Transparency** – To set the shadow's transparency.

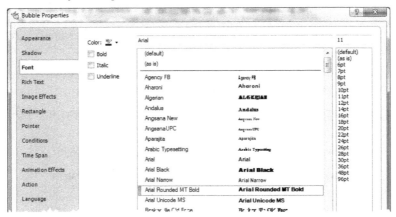

The Font tab lets you specify the font attributes for all text in the callout. If you want to assign different attributes to different pieces of text in the same callout, use the Rich Text tab instead. (You can also use the Rich Text tab to insert the initial text.) All the options on this tab should be self-explanatory.

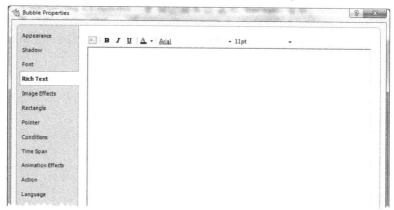

The Rich Text tab lets you add the initial text to the callout, or apply different font attributes to different words. (If you want to apply the same attributes to all the text, use the Font tab.) All the options should be self-explanatory except the first, which lets you insert a variable in the text. Variables are covered in the Advanced Features chapter.

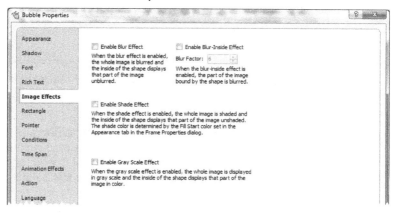

The Image Effects tab lets you apply three different effects to the callout box and the frame:

- **... Blur Effect** — To blur the entire frame except the callout box.

- **... Blur-Inside Effect** — To blur the inside of the call-out box but leave the rest of the image clear. The opposite of Blur.

- **... Shade Effect** — To shade the entire frame except the callout box.

- **... Gray Scale Effect** — To convert the entire frame to gray except the callout box.

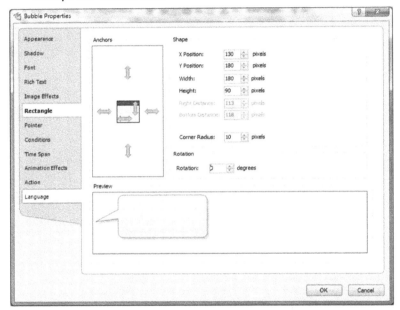

The Rectangle tab lets you set the attributes of the callout box and arrow. (You can also change these settings by moving or resizing the callout box itself.)

- **Anchors** – To "lock" the distance between objects in the box and the edges of the box so that they keep their position if you resize or crop the box. You can control the distance by using the Right Distance and Bottom Distance options, discussed below.

- **Shape – X Position/Y Position** — To set the coordinates of the upper left corner of the box.

- **Width/Height** — To set the box's width and height in pixels from its upper left corner.

- **Right Distance/Bottom Distance** — To set the related anchor distance, if you use those anchors.

- **Corner Radius** – To set the curvature of the box corners. The higher the number, the rounder.

- **Rotation** – To rotate the callout box. A positive number rotates it clockwise, negative rotates it counterclockwise.

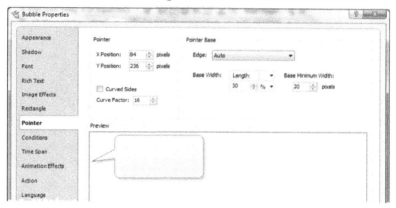

The Pointer tab lets you set the attributes of the callout box's pointer arrow.

- **Pointer – X Position/Y Position** — To set the coordinates of the tip of the pointer arrow.

- **Curved Sides** – To change the pointer to curved.

- **Curve Factor** — To set the degree of curve. Positive numbers curve to the left, negative to the right.

- **Pointer Base-Edge** — The edge of the callout box on which to anchor the pointer. The Auto option automatically uses the best-fitting edge.

- **Base Width** — The width of the arrow base, defaulting to a % of the callout box length. Also specifiable in points, pixels, centimeters, millimeters, inches, picas, ems, and exes.

    Tip – You can leave this set to % to use a relative setting for the width, or use Ems. Exes are not well supported by browsers.

- **Base Minimum Width** – To set a minimum size for the pointer base no matter what base width setting you use.

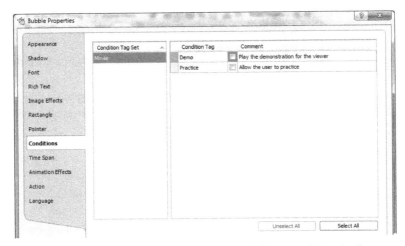

The Conditions tab lets you apply an existing condition to the callout box. (To define, edit, or delete a condition, see the section on Conditions in the Advanced Features chapter.)

- **Condition Tag Set** — To pick the set containing the desired tag, if you have multiple sets. Otherwise, lists the default set.

- **Condition Tag** – Lists the tags in the selected tag set. Click in the check box for the desired tag to apply it to this callout.

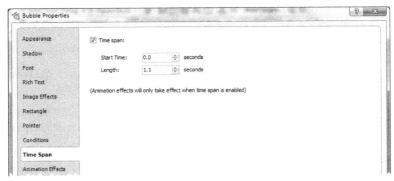

The Time Span tab lets you set the start time and duration of the callout. You can also change these settings through the timeline.

- **Start Time** — The time at which to start displaying the callout box.

- **Length** — The amount of time to display the callout box.

Note – You must enable the time span in order for animation effects to work.

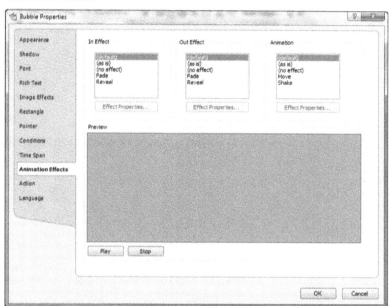

The Animation Effects tab lets you set animation effects for the callout box. You can define how the box appears or disappears, such as a fade in and out, and any effects to play while the box displays, such as shaking.

- **In Effect** — The effect to play as the box appears. You can select from a fade in, a reveal (in which the box slides in), the default (no effect unless you added the box to the palette and specified an effect there), as is, or no effect.

- **Out Effect** — The effect as the box closes. Same options as In Effect.

  Each option's Effect Properties button opens a dialog box where you can set the direction and duration of the effect.

- **Animation** — The effect while the box is displayed. You can select from a move in which the box moves along a path (defined by clicking on the box, clicking the Trajectory Mode icon ⬚ on the Frame toolbar, and dragging the box to its end point), a shake (in which the box shakes up and/or down a specified number of times per second), the default (no effect unless you added the box to the palette and specified an effect there), as is, or no effect.

Each Effect Properties button displays a dialog box where you can specify the direction and duration of the effect.

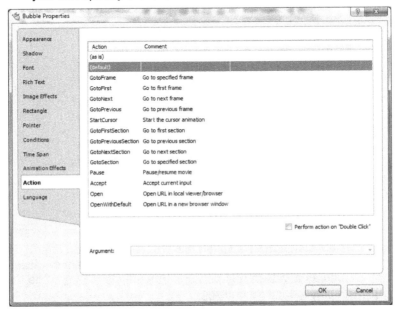

The Action tab lets you specify what happens when the viewer clicks the box. The options are largely self-explanatory. Click the ? icon in the upper right corner of the box and click the link in the first bullet (Action (Action Tab)) for an explanation of the options.

If you select GoToFrame, you must specify the frame name in the argument field. This means you must assign a text name to the frame. To do so, enter it in the Frame Name field on the Appearance tab of the Frame Properties dialog box.

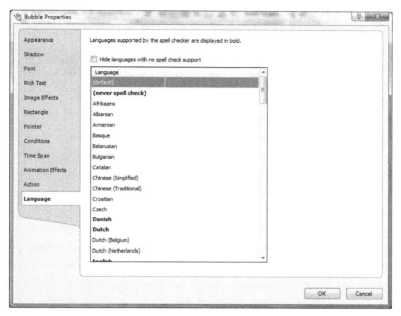

The Language tab lets you specify the language for the object to:

- Set the language that the spell-checker will use.

- Set the language for navigation element captions like the Back button, if you're publishing the output in Flash, AIR, or Silverlight format.

Mimic's spell-checker supports languages in bold . The Hide... option hides languages that the spell-checker does not support.

4. When you finish making the settings, click **OK**.

Tip – The arrow's base moves around the callout's sides as you drag the tip.

5. Select **Save All**.

Highlight Boxes

A highlight box is a rectangle, circle, or polygon (irregular shape) that you draw around an area of the screen for visual emphasis. For example, if a frame contains a feature that's important but doesn't stand out visually, you can add a highlight box that displays at the same time as a callout that describes the feature.

Here's an example of a highlight box, the red (if viewed online) box around the base options on the left side of the frame.

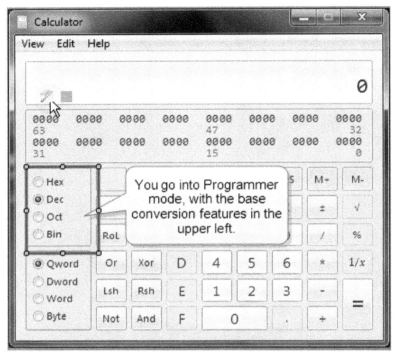

Whether you create rectangular, circular, or polygonal highlight boxes, you'll use almost the same options. Those options are also nearly the same as the options for callouts. Because of the similarities, this book won't show the screens from the callout section again and will discuss specific highlight options only as they differ for the rectangle, circle, or polygon. The table below lists the tabs available for each type.

The rectangle, oval, and polygon options are available from the pulldown on the Mode icon on the toolbar, just to the left of the Trajectory Mode icon. Note that this icon always shows the last option used; if you last used the oval option, the icon displays an oval instead of a rectangle.

Tab	Bubble	Rectangle	Oval	Polygon
Appearance	✓	✓	✓	✓
Shadow	✓	✓	✓	✓
Font	✓	✓	✓	✓
Rich Text	✓	✓	✓	✓
Zoom Effect		✓		
Image Effects	✓	✓	✓	✓
Rectangle	✓	✓	✓	
Pointer	✓			
Conditions	✓		✓	✓
Time Span	✓	✓	✓	✓
Animation Effects	✓	✓	✓	✓
Action	✓	✓	✓	✓
Language	✓	✓	✓	✓

To create a highlight box:

1. Display the frame on which to add a highlight box.

2. Select Rectangle, Oval, or Polygon Mode from the Mode icon pulldown.

   The pointer changes to a small cross-hair.

3. Click in the frame, hold the left mouse button down, and drag out a rectangle, oval, or polygon around the area to highlight.

To create a polygon, move the pointer icon to the start position, click and hold down the mouse button and drag the pointer until you get to a turn point. Then release the mouse button, click it and hold it down again, and drag to the next turn point. Repeat until you've drawn out the polygon. Then double click.

The image below shows the rectangle, oval, and polygon shape.

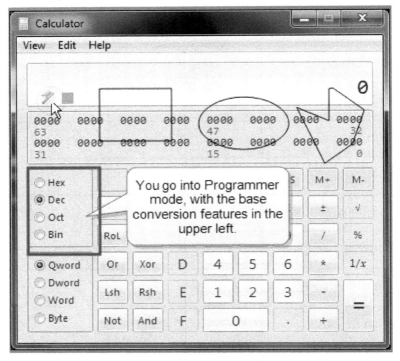

Notice the grab handles on the corners and sides of the rectangle and oval and at the turn points of the polygon. Click on and drag any of the grab handles to resize the highlight. Click inside the highlight and drag to move it.

4. To set the highlight's properties, double click on it. The Rectangle, Oval, or Polygon Properties dialog box opens, with the appropriate tabs.

The tabs are very similar for each option. The main difference is the Zoom Effect tab for a rectangular highlight box.

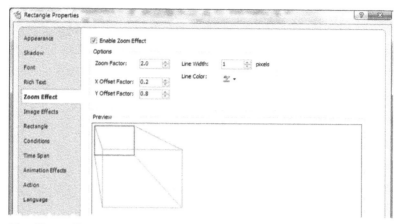

The Zoom Effect tab lets you add a zoom feature to the highlight box, like holding a magnifying glass over the image:

- **Zoom Factor** — The magnification level.

- **X/Y Offset Factor** — The amount by which the magnified image is offset horizontally and vertically from the base image.

- **Line Width** — The thickness of the lines of the magnification box.

- **Line Color** – The color of the lines of the 3-D box that emerges from the magnification area.

4. When you finish making the settings, click **OK**.

Loops

A loop is like a free-hand circle drawn around part of the screen for visual emphasis, like a highlight box but with a freehand look. For example, if a frame contains a feature that's important but doesn't stand out visually, you can add a loop that displays at the same time as a callout that describes the feature.

Here's an example of a loop, the "hand-drawn" oval around the base options on the left side of the frame.

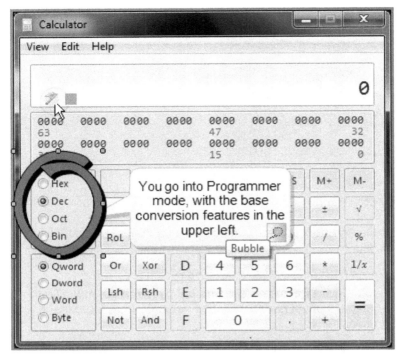

Loop options are similar to those for highlight boxes. Because of this, the book only describes loop options that differ from those of highlight boxes.

To create a loop:

1. Display the frame on which to add a loop.

2. Select the Loop Mode icon from the toolbar.

    The pointer changes to a small cross-hair.

3. Click in the frame, hold the left mouse button down, and drag out a box the size of the loop around the area to highlight.

    Notice the grab handles at the corners and edges of the box

    Click on and drag any of the grab handles to resize the loop. Click on the loop border and drag to move it.

5. To set the loop properties, double click it. The Loop Properties dialog box opens. Most of the tabs are identical to those for highlight boxes, except for Loop.

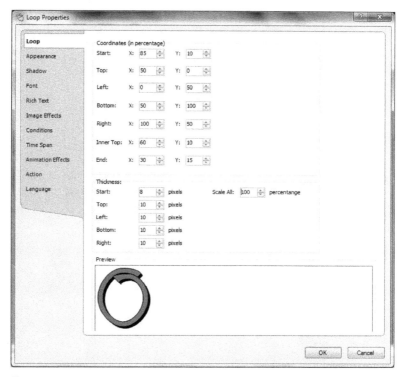

The Loop tab lets you control the location and thickness of each part of the loop – the starting tail, the top, left, bottom, and right parts of the curve, the inner portion of the top, and the ending tail. For example, compare the loop in the preview above with the one below, with the Start coordinates changed from 85/10 to 65/40.

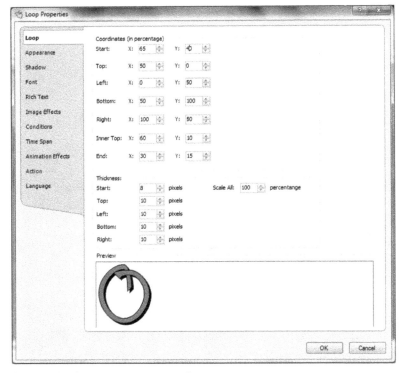

For each element, you can select:

- **X/Y Coordinate** — To set the coordinates of that part of the loop.

- **Thickness** — To set the thickness of each part of the loop.

- **Scale All** – To set the thickness of all parts at once.

4. When you finish making the settings, click **OK**.

Arrows

Arrows are straight or curved lines with a head and tail. You'll typically use them to point to an object on the screen for emphasis.

Here's an example, the double arrow pointing to the bottom of the base options area. Note that the right-hand arrow has two legs. This type of arrow, called a "polyline," is made up of one or more straight line legs.

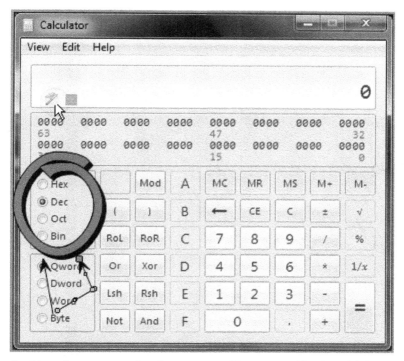

And here's an example of an arrow with a curved body, which you create using Mimic's arrow mode.

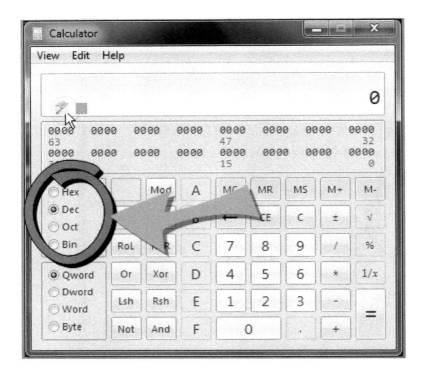

Creating Straight-Line Arrows

Most of the options are the same as those for callouts or highlights, so we'll only cover those options specific to straight-line arrows.

1. Display the frame on which to add an arrow.

2. Select Polyline Mode from the Mode icon pulldown on the toolbar.

   The pointer changes to a small pen-point.

3. Click where you want the line to start, hold the left mouse button down, and drag out the arrow body line.

   To create a polyline, a line with multiple segments, move the pointer icon to the start position, click and hold down the mouse button and drag the pointer until you get to the end of the first segment. Then release the mouse button, click it and hold it down again, and drag to the end of the next segment. Repeat until you've drawn out the polyline. Then double click.

The image below shows two lines – the single leg line on the left and the multi-segment line on the right.

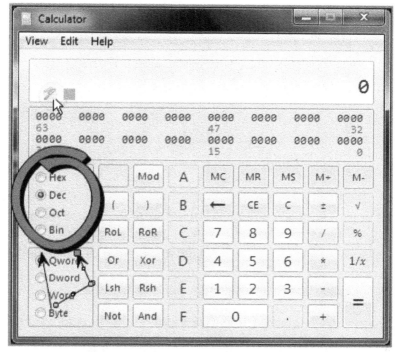

Notice the grab handles on the ends and centers of each leg.

Click on and drag any of the grab handles to move or reshape the line.

4. To set the arrow's properties, double click on it. The Polyline Properties dialog box opens.

    The tabs are almost identical to the Bubble properties tabs. The main difference is the presence of the Arrows tab.

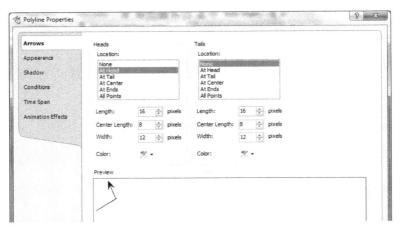

The Arrows tab lets you define the arrow attributes:

- **Heads** — Where to put the arrow head(s), and their length, width, and color.

- **Tails** — Where to put the arrow tail(s), and their length, width, and color.

4. When you finish making the settings, click **OK**.

Creating Curved-Line Arrows

The curved line arrow feature lets you add more artistic arrows. Most of the options are the same as those used for callouts, so we'll only cover those options specific to curved-line arrows.

1. Display the frame on which to add an arrow.

2. Click the Arrow mode icon ![icon] on the toolbar.

    The pointer changes to a small cross-hair.

3. Click where you want the line to start, hold the left mouse button down, and drag out the line to the tip.

    The arrow displays, with the tail compressed into the head and two grab handles, one on the head and one on the tail. Click on either grab handle and drag to extend the head or tail and "open up" the arrow. Click on the arrow body and drag to move it.

4. To set the arrow's properties, double click on it. The Arrow Properties dialog box opens.

    The tabs are similar to the Bubble properties tabs. The main difference is the presence of the Arrow tab.

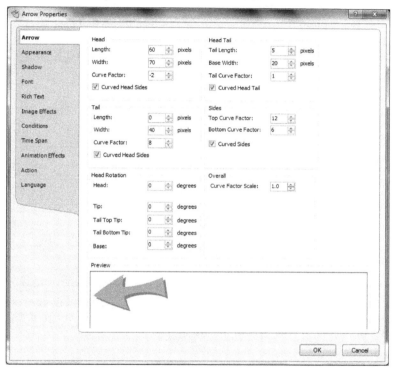

The Arrow tab lets you set the arrow shape attributes. Each option has the same, self-explanatory properties.

- **Length** — The length of the option.

- **Width** — The width of the option.

- **Curve Factor** – The amount of curvature to apply to the object. Negative and positive entries apply the curvature in different directions.

- **Head Rotation** – The amount of rotation to apply to specific parts of the arrow.

5. When you finish making the settings, click **OK**.

Rollovers

Rollovers have two parts, a hotspot and a popup that displays when viewers move the mouse over the hotspot. The screen below shows the *developer view* of a frame with hotspots over each base option in Windows' XP calculator and the popup that displays when viewers hover over each option. In viewer mode, only one popup displays at a time.

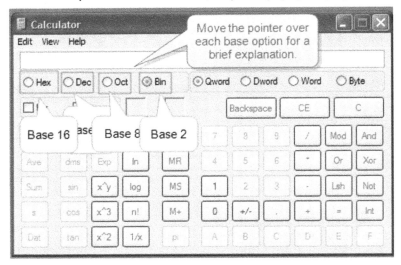

Note that there's also a callout with instructions. Without it, viewers might not know what to do on this screen. Here's what viewers see if the pointer is on the Hex option, for example:

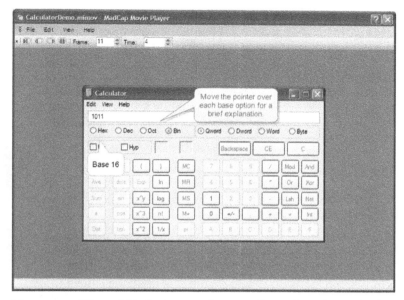

The popup "Base 16" displays as long as the pointer is on the hotspot. Move the pointer off the hotspot and the popup closes.

Tip – You *can* use callouts instead of rollovers, but showing four callouts at once clutters the screen. Some viewers may not want all that detail. If they know all the bases except Hex, why force them to see definitions of the others? With rollovers, viewers see just what they want for as long as they want by rolling over the hot spot. Just be sure to tell them what to do.

Note – Rollovers are text-only.

The easiest way to create rollovers is to mark the hotspot, then create and assign the caption. You'll also find that creating rollovers uses features that, for the most part, are discussed in previous sections. Mimic is easy to learn because it re-uses the same features in different ways.

To create a rollover:

1. Display the frame on which to add the rollover.

2. Select Rectangle, Oval, or Polygon Mode and draw the hover area. The hover area is usually rectangular but doesn't have to be.

    The pointer changes to a small cross-hair.

3. Click in the frame and drag out the hover shape. If you want to create a rectangle or oval, just click the mouse pointer, hold it down, and drag.

To create a polygon, move the pointer to the start position, click and hold down the mouse button and drag the pointer until you get to a turn point. Release the mouse button, click and hold it again, and drag to the next turn point. Repeat as needed, then double click.

Now add the popup.

4. Click on the pulldown for the Button Mode icon and select Rollover Caption Mode.

5. Click the mouse pointer roughly where you want the callout box's upper left corner to be, hold the mouse button down, and drag out a roughly-sized callout box. The box displays, with the pointer arrow pointing roughly toward the hotspot. You can size and position the callout box.

Double-click on the callout box to display the Rollover Caption Properties dialog box. Its tabs are identical to those for a callout.

6. Type the popup caption text, modify any other attributes as needed, and position the box and pointer arrows by clicking on the box and/or icon in the lower right corner and dragging it.

Here's a sample rollover for the Sin, Cos, and Tan buttons.

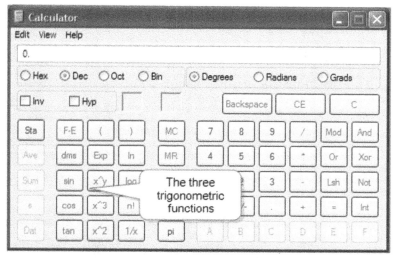

7. When you finish making the settings, click **OK**.

Tip – Note that there's no hotspot border in the example. Borders show viewers where to hover but clutter the screen, especially if there are a lot of hotspots. To avoid this, make the hotspot border invisible. Double-click the hotspot, select the Appearance tab, and set the Line Width to 0. (Tell the viewers, via a callout, that there *are* hotspots on the screen.)

Adding and Manipulating Frames

A raw movie contains just the frames captured in the initial recording. You can easily add frames for use as a title or copyright page, for example, and change the sequence and properties of all the frames.

Adding and Resequencing Frames

To add a frame, select a frame on the Frames pane *after which* to add the new one, then add the new one. For example, to add a new frame in position 3, select frame 2 and add the new one. It appears in position 3.

Note – You can add new frames from the Frame editor or the Frames pane. The steps are the same.

To add a frame:

1. Click on the frame after which to add the new frame.

   If the Frames pane is not displayed, select **View > Frames**. If the

Frames toolbar is not displayed, select **View > Toolbars > Frames**.

2. Select **Insert > Blank Frame** or click the Insert a Blank Frame After the Current One icon 📁.

In addition to this option, you can also:

- Click the Insert a Frame Using the Same Bitmap After the Selected One icon 🖼 to add a new frame that contains the same bitmap as the current frame.

  This creates a link from the bitmap in the new frame to the bitmap in the selected frame. Changing the bitmap in the selected frame changes the bitmap in the new frame. If you move the new frame to a new position in the movie, its bitmap will change if you change the bitmap in the frame that now precedes it.

- Click the Insert PowerPoint... icon 🖼 to select a PowerPoint file and specific slides in that file.

  If the PowerPoint slides have graphic objects like text boxes, selecting the Import Slides as Background... option offers higher quality graphics but you can't edit the objects in Mimic. (This assumes that you edited the objects as desired in PowerPoint.) Deselect the Import Slides... option to edit those objects in Mimic.

- Click the Record New Frames... *button* to minimize Mimic and open a capture box the same size as the original. You can then record new frames and insert them directly after the frame where you clicked the Record New Frames button. Basically, this option lets you add *multiple* frames to a movie.

- Click the Capture New Frame... *button* to minimize Mimic and open a capture box the same size as the original. You can then capture a screen shot and insert it in a new frame that Mimic adds directly after the frame where you clicked the Capture New Frame button. Basically, this option lets you add *one* frame to a movie.

78

3. If the new frame is in the wrong position, click on it on the Frames pane. (Select **View > Frames** if you don't see the Frames pane.) Then click the up or down arrow on the Frames pane toolbar, shown below, to move the frame.

Editing Frame Properties

You can modify a frame's properties.

To edit frame properties:

1. Click on the frame whose properties you want to edit.

2. Select **Frames > Frame Properties** or click the Edit Frame

   Properties icon ⌨.

   The Frame Properties dialog box opens.

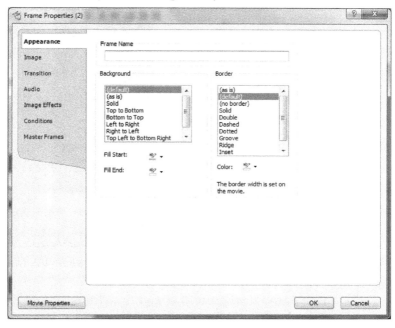

The Appearance tab lets you set the frame's box's basic label, color, and border values:

- **Frame Name**— To give the frame a descriptive title. Viewers don't see this title. It displays in the Frames pane in place of the frame number. You don't have to specify a name. But if you use any interactive features that can branch to different frames, you must assign textual names to the target frames.

- **Background** — To set the frame's background color as solid or as a color gradient in different directions.

- **Fill Start/Fill End** — To set the starting and ending colors for a gradient.

- **Border** – To set the border style for the frame.

- **Color** – To set the frame's border color.

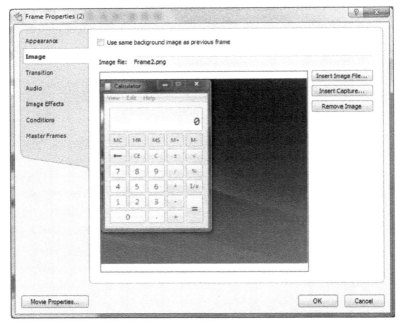

The Image tab lets you add a new image to use as the frame background or change the image:

- **Use Same Background image...** — To replace any image in this frame with the one from the previous frame.

- **Insert Image...** — To insert an image in this frame. You can select BMP, GIF, JPG, JPEG, TIF, TIFF, or PNG files.

- **Insert Capture...** — To minimize Mimic in order to capture a new image, which Mimic then uses as the background for the frame.

- **Remove Image...** — To remove the existing image from the frame, leaving the frame blank.

- **Movie Properties button** — To open the Movie Properties dialog box.

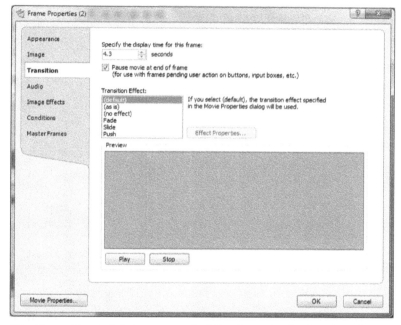

The Transition tab lets you control the frame's display duration (ignoring the duration of any objects on the frame), and the transition from one frame to another:

- **... Display Time...** — To set the duration in tenths of a second.

- **Pause Movie...** — To pause the movie at the end of this frame rather than automatically continuing to the next frame.

    Tip – Use this if you add a user-clickable button or click box to a frame and want the movie to pause until the user clicks.

- **Transition Effect** — To specify the transition effect between frames.

- **Effect Properties** — To specify the properties of a transition effect. The Effect Properties dialog box is the same for each effect.

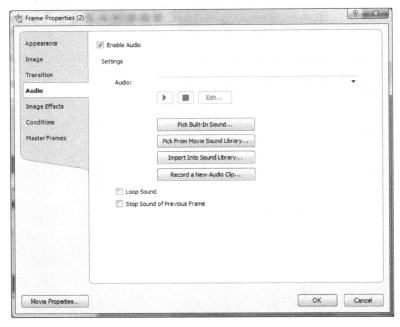

The Audio tab lets you add audio to a frame by importing an existing audio clip or recording a new one:

- **Enable Audio** – Turns on the audio options.

- **Play, Pause** — To play or pause the selected audio file.

- **Edit** — To open the audio editor for an audio file that you recorded. This is disabled for audio files that ship with Mimic.

- **Pick Built-In...** — To use one of the audio files that ships with Mimic.

- **Pick From... Library** — To re-use a clip already imported into the movie and now in the sound library. This reduces the movie size since you're not adding another sound file.

- **Import Into... Library** — To import an external audio clip in WAV or MP3 format into the movie.

- **Record a New Audio Clip** — Self-explanatory.

- **Loop Sound** — To loop the clip repeatedly until the end of the frame. This eliminates the need to find a clip whose duration matches that of the frame. You may hear a pause as the loop re-starts. This is due to an MP3 peculiarity.

- **Stop Sound of Previous Frame** — To stop playing any audio from the previous frame in order to avoid interference between the two clips. This option is not available for object or movie audio.

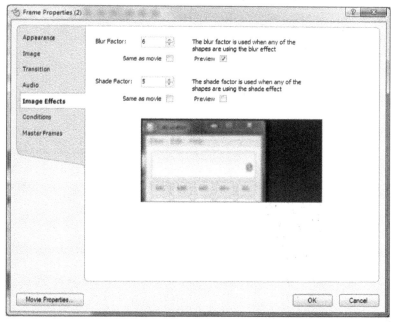

The Image Effects tab lets you set the amount of blur or shade on the frame, *if you turn on the blur or shade effect for an object on the frame.* To set the degree of blur or shade for the entire movie, use the Movie Properties dialog box's Image Effects tab

- **Blur Factor** — To increase or decrease the blur. The higher the number, the greater the blur.

- **Shade Factor** — To increase or decrease the shading. The higher the number, the greater the shading.

- **Same as Movie** — To use the blur or shade setting of the overall movie.

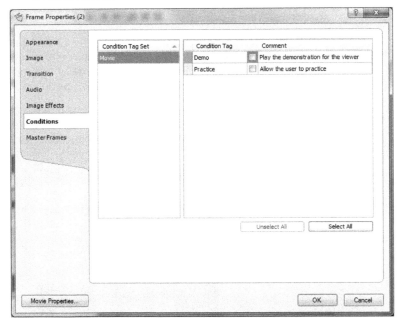

The Conditions tab lets you apply existing conditions to the frame. It's identical to the Conditions tab for Bubble Properties.

The Master Frames tab lets you select a master frame to use as an under- or overlay. See the Advanced Features chapter.

3. When you finish making the settings, click **OK**.

Adding and Manipulating Images

You can add images to your frames for many reasons, such as:

- Adding a different background.

- Using your company's logo as a watermark.

- Creating movies that focus on role-playing, such as sales training, rather than software training. For example, you can add a photo of a person at a decision point with two options from which to choose. Each option might take viewers to a different part of the movie or different movies.

After adding an image, you can set its duration, transparency, delay, what to do if the viewer clicks on it, and more. You can insert images in bmp, jpg, jpeg, gif, png, tif, tiff, or cur (cursor) format.

Adding Images

Adding an image is simple – insert the image, then modify its settings.

1. Click on the frame on which to add the image.

2. Select **Insert > Image**.

   The Open dialog box opens.

3. Select the image to insert and click **Open**.

Moving or Resizing Images

You can move and resize an image manually or by using a dialog box.

To move and resize an image manually:

1. Click on the image.

   Grab handles display on each corner and in the middle of each side.

2. To move the image, click inside the image, hold the mouse button down, and drag.

   To resize the image *non-proportionally*, click and drag any corner or side grab handle to resize the image.

To move or resize an image or add effects using a dialog box:

1. Double-click on the image.

   The Image Properties dialog box opens. The tabs are identical to those for callouts, except the Image and Edge Effects tabs, so we'll just look at those two here.

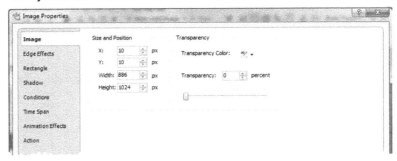

The Image tab lets you specify the image's position, size, and transparency:

- **X/Y** — The coordinates of the image's upper left corner.

- **Width/Height** — The width and height to the right and down from the upper left corner.

- **Transparency Color** — The color to apply to the image as a transparent overlay. Note that this feature is not working as of Feb. 27, 2012.

- **Transparency** — The amount of transparency, the higher the number the greater the transparency.

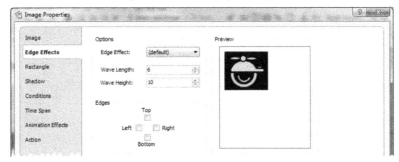

The Edge Effects tab lets you specify the effect, if any, to apply to the edge of the image:

- **Edge Effect** — The effect None (default) or Torn.

- **Wave Length** — The length from trough to trough. The lower the number, the narrower the tears.

- **Wave Height** — The height of each tear. The lower the number, the lower the tear.

- **Edges** — The edges to which to apply the effect.

2. When you finish, click **OK**.

Align Multiple Images

You can align multiple images by using the Object Layout toolbar.

1. Insert the images on the frame and align them roughly.

2. Click on the image to be the alignment anchor, then select the images to align to the anchor. For example, to align the bottom of image A to the bottom of image B, select image B first, then image A, then select the Same Bottom option from the toolbar.

3. If the Object Layout toolbar is not open, select **View > Toolbars > Layout**.

The Object Layout toolbar displays.

Select the appropriate option from this list:

Name	Description
Sink	Sends the object down one layer.
Float	Sends the object up one layer.
Sink to Bottom	Sends the object to the bottom.
Float to Top	Sends the object to the top.
Same Left	Aligns objects to the left side of the anchor.
Same Right	Aligns objects to the right side of the anchor.

Name	Description
Same Bottom	Aligns objects to the bottom of the anchor.
Same Top	Aligns objects to the top of the anchor.
Same Width	Makes objects the same width as the anchor.
Same Height	Makes objects the same height as the anchor.
Same Size	Makes objects the same width and height as the anchor.
Vertically Align On Center	Vertically aligns objects on their centers.
Horizontally Align On Center	Horizontally aligns objects on their centers.
Center... On Canvas	Centers objects on the frame.
Horizontally Center... Canvas	Centers objects horizontally on the frame.
Vertically Center... Canvas	Centers objects vertically on the frame.

Object Trajectories

When you capture frames for a new movie, Mimic automatically captures your mouse pointer movements. You can turn this off before you start if you decide not to show the pointer. (Some authors think the movement is distracting and replace it with visual emphases like highlight boxes.) Or you can capture the pointer movement but modify it after capturing it. Mimic adds additional flexibility by letting you add trajectories, or motion paths, to other objects on a frame. You can:

- Add a trajectory to an object, such as adding a path along which an image might move. This is very simple animation.

- Customize how a trajectory looks to the developer.

- Change a trajectory's path.

- Remove a trajectory from an object.

Capturing Mouse Pointer Movement

Mimic can automatically capture the pointer movement as you record.

To turn mouse pointer recording off or on:

1. Start and configure the application you want to record.

2. Switch back to Mimic.

3. Select **Movie > Record Movie** and click the **Options** icon OR

   Click the Record New Movie icon ⬤ on the toolbar and click the **Options** icon.

   The Recording Options dialog box opens.

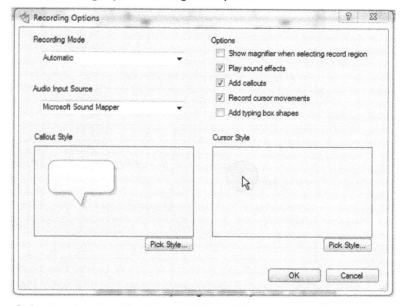

Select or deselect the Record Cursor Movements option.

4. Continue creating the new movie.

Adding a Trajectory to an Object

Adding a trajectory to an object defines its start and end points on a frame and the path in between. For example, you might place an image in the center of a title frame for visual effect, then move it into the upper left corner of the frame to keep it on the frame but out of the way visually. You'd create this effect by adding a trajectory to the object.

1. Select the object that you want to animate.

2. Select **Object > Trajectory Mode** or click the Enter... Trajectory Mode icon on the Frames toolbar, and move the pointer back on the frame.

   A copy of the object selected in step 1 displays, connected to the original object by a heavy line that indicates the trajectory.

3. Position the copy of the object where you want its motion to end and click the mouse.

   A message asks if you want to accept the trajectory.

4. Click **Yes**.

Reshaping a Trajectory

After adding a trajectory, you may decide you don't like its start or end points. You can delete and redo the trajectory, or just reshape its start or end points.

1. Select the object whose trajectory you want to reshape or move.

   If you don't see the line, click the Draw Animation Trajectories icon on the Frames toolbar.

2. To move the starting point, click on the starting object. Grab handles will display on the corners and sides. Drag that object to the new position.

   To move the ending point, click on the grab handle at the end of the trajectory line and drag it to the desired new position.

Removing a Trajectory

If you decide not to use a trajectory, you can easily remove it.

1. Select the object whose trajectory line you want to remove.

    If you don't see the trajectory line, click the Draw Animation Trajectories icon [icon] on the Frames toolbar.

2. Select **Object > Reset Trajectory**.

    The trajectory line disappears from the frame.

Note – Don't select the object and click Delete. This removes both the trajectory line and the object itself.

Object Groups

Object grouping is a convenience feature. It's similar to a multi-select but retains the multi-selected state until you command otherwise, rather than losing that state as soon as you click off the selected objects.

For example, say you want to move several callouts on a frame but keep their relative positions. Hold the Ctrl key and click on the boxes to select and move them as a group. But once you click off the boxes, they're no longer grouped. To move them as a group again, you must multi-select them again. Not a major problem, but still annoying.

Object groups fix that. Grouped objects stay grouped even after you click off them or even go to a different frame and return to the one on which you created the group. Mimic adds a box with a light gray border around a group as a visual indicator.

You can easily ungroup a set of objects to restore their individual status.

Creating An Object Group

Creating a group is the same as multi-selecting, but with one extra step at the end.

1. Press and hold down the Ctrl key and click on all the objects that you want to group.

2. Right-click on any of the selected objects and select **Group Selected Items**.

    The light gray "grouped items" box displays around the objects.

Ungrouping An Object Group

This is simple. The hardest part may be locating the group.

1. Right-click on the group and select **Ungroup Shapes**.

   The objects return to their individual status.

6 Timing Control

Mimic's timing control features let you control the display duration of frames and the objects on them.

Frame Timing

Setting frame timing is easy technically. What's hard is setting a *usable* timing. Several factors affect this:

- The number, type, and content of objects on the frame. Viewers have to see the objects, read them, understand them, possibly act on them. That may take longer than you think, which is why usability testing is useful.

  Let's say a frame has a callout. You have to make sure it stands out visually and is clearly written. You'll also have to leave time for comprehension and action. You can do that by extending the frame's duration, but for how long?

  Now say the callout tells viewers to roll the mouse over buttons in the frame. As they do, a rollover description pops up for each button. You can't predict a particular viewer's reading speed, so you have to leave time for moving around, reading, and compre-hending. You *can* extend the slide's duration, but for how long? And one viewer's rushed duration is another one's slow.

  To fix this, you could stop the automatic frame advance and add a "Click Here to Continue" button to the frame. Viewers can read at their own pace and advance when ready, without being bored or rushed. But you now have to be sure the callout box also explains the button, so the callout box takes more time to read and comprehend. This isn't hard to do; you just have to remember to do it and using which features.

- Viewer's English skill and educational level. It's hard to predict how these two attributes affect reading speed, but assume that lower English skill and educational level equals slower reading.

- The viewer's PC skill. We assume that viewers know how to use a PC but that's often not true. If you tell viewers to click a "Click Here to Continue" button to go to the next frame, will they look for the button on the screen or the keyboard? Ask tech support.

- The viewer's domain knowledge. If your movies explain how to perform some task in your software, do your viewers have the knowledge to understand the context of the instructions? For example, if you tell viewers to select a Fixed Asset Depreciation Method option from a dropdown in an accounting package, will the viewers understand the differences between the options or do you have to explain them?

Object Timing and Relationships

We often have multiple on a frame. For example, a frame may have a callout that explains a section of the frame, with a high-light box to add emphasis. The issue is how the objects' timing relates to each other. For example, if a frame has a callout and a highlight box, should they display simultaneously or should the callout display first, then the highlight box a few seconds later to add visual emphasis though a cascade of effects?

There's no one right answer. You may find some good tips in *e-Learning and the Science of Instruction: Proven Guidelines for Consumers and Designers of Multimedia Learning* by Clark and Mayer in the eLearning series from ASTD (American Society for Training and Development) at www.astd.org.

Object timing design is a complex topic, but object timing mechanics are pretty simple.

Timing Control Tools

There are two ways to control the duration of a frame and the duration and delay of an object – the Properties dialog boxes and the timeline.

Properties Dialog Box

Every object's Properties dialog box includes a Time Span tab, like the one below from the Bubble Properties dialog box.

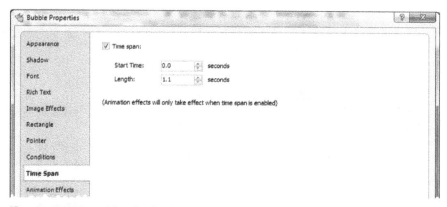

To change the object's display delay or duration, change the field values.

Tip – To set an object's timing in relation to other objects on the frame, use the timeline rather than the Time Span tab.

The Timeline

The timeline visually represents a frame and its objects. The frame and objects are on separate rows, or "layers," whose timing you can adjust while seeing them in context of other objects on the frame. For example.

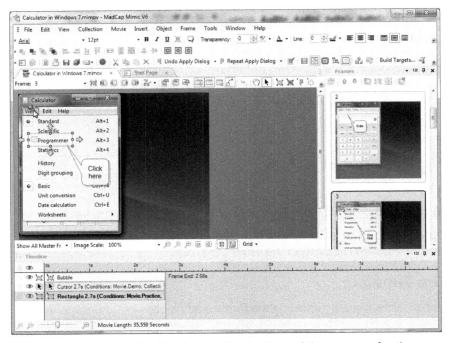

This example shows the timeline, at the bottom of the screen, for the frame shown in the working area.

The timeline offers these options:

- The lock icon "locks" an object on the timeline or all objects. This does not provide security. It's more like a speed bump that keeps you from changing an option's timing by accident until you unlock the item.

- The eye icon turns off the display of a particular object or type of object on the working area. Those items are still part of the frame but are simply hidden temporarily. Clicking the topmost eye icon hides all the objects on the screen. You can then click the eye icon for particular objects to display them only.

- The screen object icons let you select all objects of a given type on a frame.

- The magnification icons and slider let you expand or shrink the timeline if you need to see greater detail.

The sample timeline above contains three layers.

- The top layer is "Bubble." Its box starts at the left end of the time-line, 0 seconds, and goes to 2.68, so the object, a callout, opens when the frame opens and displays for 2.68 seconds.

- The next layer is "Cursor 2.7s." Its box starts at the left end of the timeline, 0 seconds, and extends to 2.7, so this object, a cursor movement, also opens when the frame opens and moves for 2.7 seconds until it reaches the click point.

- The last layer is "Rectangle 2.7s." Its box starts at the left end of the timeline, 0 seconds, and extends to 2.7, so this object, the clickable hotspot over the menu selection, also opens when the frame opens and displays for 2.7 seconds until the cursor click.

How do you tell what layer on a timeline equals what object on a frame? Clicking on a timeline layer selects the equivalent object on the frame. In the example above, clicking on the bubble layer on the timeline selects it (its color changes) and that object on the frame (the callout box) is high-lighted and displays grab handles.

Displaying the Timeline

The timeline uses a lot of space so you can close it when developing if you're not working on frame and object timing.

1. To open the timeline, select **View > Timeline** or click the Open the Timeline Window icon ⬚ on the Standard toolbar.

   The timeline window displays at the bottom of the screen. It has the same controls as any other window.

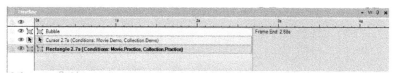

2. To close the timeline, click the x on the Timeline window title bar.

Controlling Object Display Delay and Duration

1. Display the timeline.

2. Display the frame containing the object whose timing you want to modify.

3. Select **Movie > Quick-preview Movie > This Frame** or click the

    Quick-Preview Movie icon ⚙ ▾ pulldown and select This
    Frame.

    The MadCap Movie Player displays and plays the frame. Watch
    the timing of and transitions between the objects on the frame,
    then close the preview window.

4. To change an object's display delay, click on its layer box in the
    timeline and drag the box right or left to increase or reduce the
    delay.

You can also double-click the object box to display the object's
Properties dialog box and select its Time Span tab, or click the object
and select the Display Properties icon on the timeline.

To change an object's duration, click on its layer box in the timeline, put
the pointer on either end of the box until the pointer turns into a double-
headed arrow, and drag right or left to shorten or lengthen the box,
reducing or increasing its duration.

You can also double-click on the box to display the object's Properties
dialog box and select its Time Span tab.

To change the timing relationship between multiple objects, just repeat
these steps for each object, previewing as you go until you have it right.

7 Movie-Level Features

Once you've created a movie and annotated the frames, you can specify features like what happens when the movie ends, its interface, and more.

Movie End Effects

When a movie ends, it stops at the last frame. But you can instead make it loop, start another movie, send the viewer to a URL, and more. These options add flexibility to your work.

1. Select **Movie > Movie Properties** OR click the **Movie**

    Properties icon on the Frame toolbar.

    The Movie Properties dialog box opens.

2. Click the End Action tab.

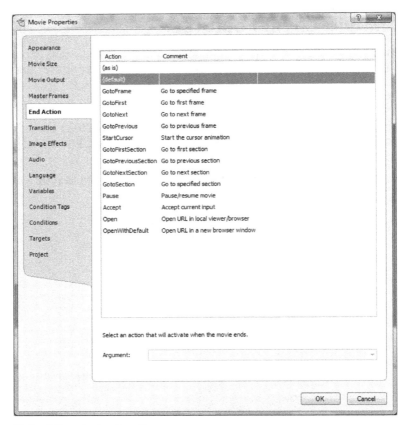

3. Select the desired action.

The bottom field changes for certain actions. For example, if you select the GoToFrame action, the field's name changes to Frame Name.

Tip – If you select the GoToFrame option, clicking the Frame Name field pulldown lists all frames to which you assigned text names but *not* frames that just use the numbers Mimic adds automatically. So add a text name to each frame or each major section frame. To add a text name, open the Frame Properties dialog box and the Appearance tab, and type the name in the Frame Name field.

4. Make any necessary entry in the Argument field.

5. Click **OK**.

Setting Other Movie Effects

The Movie Properties dialog box offers other movie-level effects aside from end effects. We'll look at some here and others in later chapters.

1. Select **Movie > Properties** OR click the **File Properties** icon on the Frame toolbar.

   The Movie Properties dialog box opens.

The Appearance tab lets you set basic color and border values for all frames in a movie. To set these attributes for specific frames, use the Frame Properties dialog box.

- **Background** — To set the background color as solid or as a gradient in different directions.

- **Fill Start/Fill End** — To set the starting and ending colors if you use a color gradient for the background.

- **Padding** – To set the blank space between the edge of the movie box and the frame content.

- **Copy Down** – To repeat your setting in the first (Left) padding field in the remaining three fields.

- **Border** – To specify the window border attributes.

- **Width** – To set the width of the movie's border.

- **Color** – To set the color of the movie's border.

The Transition tab lets you define a transition effect for frames for which you chose the default transition in the Frame Properties dialog box's Transition tab. (If you specified the default option elsewhere, this tab lets you define what that default option is.)

- **Transition Effect** — To set the effect. You can use a fade in, slide (where the new frame slides on top of the previous one), or a push (where the new frame pushes the previous one off the screen).

- **Effect Properties** — To set the effect duration and direction.

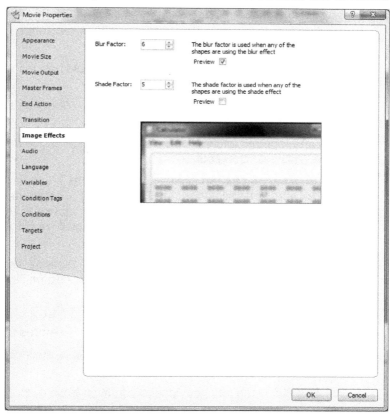

The Image Effects tab lets you set the amount of blur or shading to use for each frame that contains an object for which you turned on blur or shading in the entire movie.

- **Blur Factor** — To change the blur. The higher the number, the greater the blur.

- **Shade Factor** — To change the shading. The higher the number, the greater the shading.

The Movie Size tab lets you change the size of all the frames in the movie at once. See the Resizing Movies section later in this chapter.

The Movie Output tab lets you set the publishing options for the movie. See the Generating Output chapter.

The Master Frames tab lets you apply a frame containing standard interface elements to some or all frames in the movie. See the Advanced Features chapter.

The End Action tab lets you specify what should happen when the movie reaches the last frame.

The Audio tab lets you add audio to the movie. See the Other Features chapter.

The Language tab lets you specify the language to use for the movie. This selection sets:

- The language for the spell-checker, such as a version to deal with national variations. For example, Canadians who use English (United States) will get errors for words like colour or centre. Selecting English (Canadian) or English fixes this problem

- Sets the language for navigation element captions, like the Back button, if you plan to output in Flash, AIR, or Silverlight format.

The Variables tab lets you create and define variables for use in a movie. See the Advanced Frame Annotation Features chapter.

The Condition Tags tab lets you create and define new condition tags. See the Advanced Features chapter.

The Conditions tab lets you apply a condition to an output target, movie, or collection. See the Advanced Features chapter.

The Targets tab lets you create and define targets – outputs for specific clients, products, etc. Say you create a Flash movie for client A. You name it Flash_ movie_for_client_A and specify the mix of variables, conditions, and other settings needed to tailor it for client A. You're then asked to modify the movie so that it can be sold to client B. You make a copy of the movie, name it Flash_movie_for_client_B, and specify a mix of variables, conditions, and other settings needed to tailor the output for client B. And again for C, etc. This is single sourcing of movies using Mimic. (If you use Flare, you'll find that its target feature is conceptually identical to Mimic's.) See the Generating Output chapter.

The Project tab lets you link the movie to a Flare project in order to use the conditions and variables defined in the Flare project in the Mimic movie as well. Effectively, this programmatically links Mimic and Flare. See the Advanced Features chapter.

2. Make the desired settings.

3. Click **OK**.

Working with Skins

A skin defines the look of a movie interface the same way a cell phone faceplate defines the look of the phone. However, a faceplate just changes the look but a skin can add functionality.

You can create a skin if you're generating Flash, AIR, or Silverlight. If you're generating MadCap Mimic, PDF, or XPS, you won't create a skin since they have predefined settings.

There are two skin types – regular and language. The latter displays navigational element captions in non-English languages.

Tip – Try to define your skins before you start creating movies. This helps ensure a consistent interface among multiple movies.

Creating and Defining a Standard skin

1. Select **Movie > Properties**.

   The Movie Properties dialog box opens.

2. Select the Movie Output tab.

3. Click the Edit Skin button or the Edit Embedded Skin button for Flash or AIR. (If the button is grayed out, make sure the output, in the Default Output list at the top of the tab, is Flash or AIR.)

   The Skin Editor dialog box opens.

4. Make the desired entries in these tabs and dialog boxes. (For a Flash embedded skin, see the section of Creating and Defining an Embedded Skin.)

The Basic tab lets you specify where to put the toolbar and progress bar and whether to import or export a skin.

- **Toolbar at Top/Toolbar at Bottom** — To specify the location of the toolbar on the movie window.

- **Center Screen Progress Bar** — Displays a progress bar as the movie loads and centers the bar on the frame rather than in the navigation toolbar. For Silverlight and Flash output.

- **Import Skin** — Displays the Pick Skin dialog box, below.

- **Export Skin** — Displays the Save Skin dialog box, below.

This dialog box lets you select from a set of predefined skins, or one of your own.

- **Template folders** – Factory Templates lists templates that ship with Mimic. My Templates lists any custom templates that you defined.

- **Templates** – The template to apply to the movie.

- **Source File** – The selected template's location and file name, which has a .miskn extension.

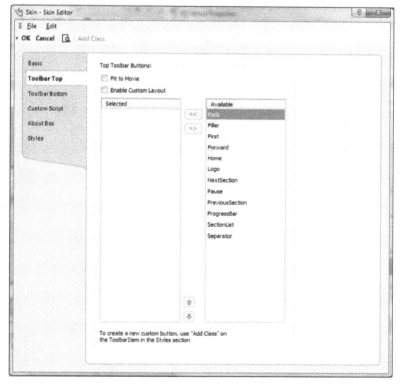

The Toolbar Top tab lets you define the toolbar controls to display at the top of the movie window.

- **Fit to Movie** – Select this option to make the toolbar width equal to that of the movie frame. Deselecting this option makes the toolbar equal to the full width of the screen. This can look odd if the movie frame is narrower than the screen.

- **Enable Custom Layout** – Select this option to turn on the features in this dialog box.

- **Available** – The predefined controls from which to select. Select the desired control from the list and click the left arrow button to add the control to the Selected list.

- **Sequence arrows** – To change the sequence of the controls in the Selected list, and thus their sequence in the toolbar.

Toolbar Bottom is identical to Toolbar Top, except that controls selected on this tab display at the bottom of the movie window. You can have the same or different toolbars at the top and bottom of the movie window at the same time.

Note – You can add a custom button if you need functionality beyond the built-in buttons.

If you create a custom toolbar button, it displays in the list of controls in the Available list box. See Creating a Custom Toolbar Item later in this chapter.

The Custom Script tab lets you add a Javascript for a custom toolbar button. Basically, this feature lets you create a custom button to do almost anything.

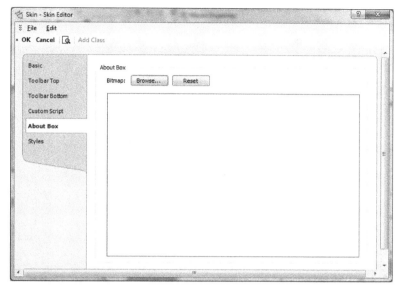

The About Box tab lets you specify an image to display if viewers click on an icon that you add to the toolbar with the Toolbar Top or Bottom tabs. You might add your company logo to the toolbar as an icon that, when clicked, opens a larger image of the logo.

- **Browse** – To find the image to display.
- **Reset** – To restore the default image.

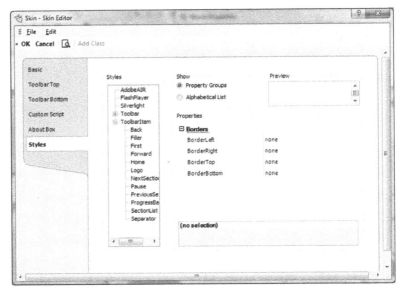

The Styles tab lets you set the attributes for the Flash, AIR, or Silverlight movie box, the upper and lower tool-bars, and the toolbar items.

If you want to add a custom toolbar item, do so here – click the ToolbarItem heading in the Styles, click the AddClass button on the toolbar, and name and define the item using the properties in the Properties list.

5.   Click the **OK** button at the top of the Skin Editor.

Creating and Defining an Embedded Skin for Flash

An embedded skin is conceptually the same as a regular skin, but Mimic offers different settings and merges them with the movie.

1.   Select **Movie > Properties**.

   The Movie Properties dialog box opens.

2.   Select the Movie Output tab.

3.   Click the Edit Embedded Skin button.

   The Embedded Skin Options dialog box opens.

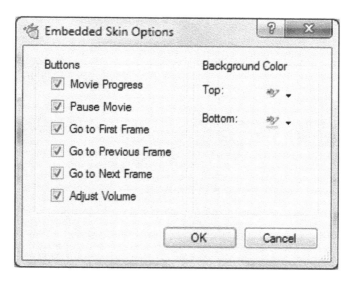

This dialog box lets you select the buttons for the toolbar and the colors.

Creating a Custom Toolbar Item

This section explains how to add a custom toolbar item, like a button that links to a web page. Custom items are controlled by Javascripts. You can create any type of custom item, each using its own Javascript, so MadCap only provides pre-defined Javascripts for basic toolbar items. If you want to add a custom item, the easiest thing is to hire a programmer.

1. Select **Movie > Properties**.

    The Movie Properties dialog box opens.

2. Select the Movie Output tab.

3. Click the Edit Skin button.

    The Skin Editor dialog box opens.

4. Click the Styles tab.

5. Click on **ToolbarItem** in the Styles list and click the Add Class button on the toolbar OR click on ToolbarItem, right-click on it, and select Add Class.

    The New Style dialog box opens.

6. Type the new item's name and click OK.

    The item displays highlighted in the ToolbarItem list.

7. Expand the desired Properties group and make the desired settings.

    To specify the Javascript, expand the Type properties group and click in the entry field for the OnClick property.

8. Click the Toolbar Top or Toolbar Bottom tab.

    The new control displays in the Available list box.

9. Add the new control to the top and/or bottom toolbar.

10. Click the **OK** button at the top of the Skin Editor.

Customizing the About Icon and Popup on the Toolbar

When you run a movie with a skin, you'll see a MadCap icon on the right end of the toolbar. Clicking on this icon opens a popup window with the MadCap logo and copyright. You can change the icon and the popup window, replacing them with small and large versions of your company's logo, for example.

1. Select **Movie > Movie Properties**.

    The Movie Properties dialog box opens.

2. Select the Movie Output tab.

3. Click the Edit Skin button. (If the button is grayed out, make sure that the output, in the Default Output list at the top of the tab, is set to Flash, AIR, or Silverlight.)

    The Skin Editor dialog box opens. You'll first specify the image that displays in the popup window when viewers click the About icon on the toolbar.

4. Click the About Box tab.

5. Click the Browse button and select the desired image.

    The image displays in the preview area. Now specify the About icon to display on the toolbar.

6. Click the Styles tab.

7. Click on **Logo** under ToolbarItem.

8. Expand the desired Properties groups and make the desired settings.

   Tip - The height of the icon image you use, set by the Icon option under the Basic property group, should be similar to the height of the toolbar so as not to make the toolbar weirdly high.

9. Click the Preview icon on the Skin Editor toolbar and check your results.

10. Close the preview.

11. Click **OK** to close the Skin Editor.

Language Skins

To fully localize a movie, you have to modify the content (text on frames and text annotations like callouts) and the interface (toolbar item labels).

Mimic uses "language skins", customizations of the Style settings you'd normally define on the Skin Editor, to localize toolbar item labels. You'll still define all the settings using the Skin Editor except the Style settings, which you define using the Language Skin Editor. Like regular skins, language skins only apply when you create the Flash, AIR, or Silverlight output.

Mimic ships with preset language skins for major European languages and variants, such as three versions of Portuguese – general, Brazilian, and Portuguese. If you need one for another language, you can create your own. See the Editing Language Skins topic in the help.

How does Mimic use skins? When you create the output, Mimic checks the Skin Editor for any manually entered settings (that override the default skin settings). If it does not find any, it checks the Language Skin Editor for manually entered settings. If it does not find any, it uses the default skin settings. So, the skin setting priorities are:

1. Manually entered settings on the Skin Editor, that override...

2. Manually entered settings on the Language Skin Editor, that override...

3. The default settings on the regular Skin Editor.

You'll just look at the Language Skin Editor here.

Opening the Language Skin Editor for a Pre-defined Language:

1. Select **Tools > Manage Language Skins.**

   The Language Skins dialog box opens.

Languages in bold have skins defined. The others don't but you can add them. (See the Editing Language Skins topic in the help.) Language skins created by the author, rather than by MadCap, display in italics in the list.

2. Select the language whose settings you want to modify, then click the Open File for Editing button.

   The language opens in the Language Skin Editor. The sample

below shows the editor open to French, with the Basic properties expanded for the Back – "Retour" in French – toolbar item.

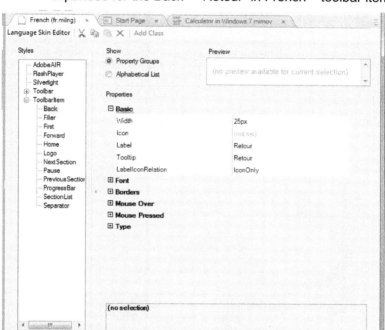

3. Make the desired settings.

Spell-Checking

You can spell check the current movie, all movies in a collection, or all open movies. As the spell-checker flags words, you can select an alternative spelling, ignore the spelling warning once or in all the files you're checking, or add the word to the dictionary.

1. Open the movie or collection to check.

2. Select **Tools > Spell Check Window** OR press **F7**

   The Spell Check window displays, highlights the first error it finds, displays a list of alternatives at the bottom of the Spell Check window, and displays the editing pane for the object containing the misspelled or unrecognized word to let you change it there.

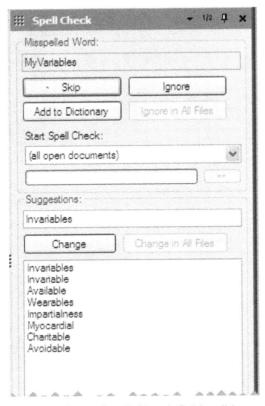

3. Click the **Start Spell Check** field pulldown and select either:

   - **Current document** — To check the currently open document.

   - **All open documents** — To check all open documents.

4. To change the spelling, select a suggestion and click **Change**. If you're checking more than the current document, click **Change in All Files** to change the spelling in all of the files.

   To keep the word as it is, click one of these buttons:

   - **Skip** — To ignore the word and move to the next misspelled word.

   - **Add to Dictionary** — To add the word to the dictionary and go to the next misspelled word.

- **Ignore** — To ignore the word and go to the next misspelled word. Also ignores other occurrences of the word in <u>this</u> document.

- **Ignore in All Files** — To ignore the spelling of the word in <u>all</u> open documents and move to the next misspelled word.

5. When the spell check ends, click **OK**.

Resizing a Movie

Before starting to create movies, determine the lowest monitor resolution that the viewers have. This is important because:

- Movies must fit on their screens without being so large that Windows adds vertical and horizontal scroll bars. Scroll bars make movies hard to use because viewers may not want to scroll or even realize they have to.

- You need a standard size for all movies from all authors. If not, viewers who go from movie to movie may find that each one is a different size. This is annoying and can cause the scroll bar problem.

We often assume that 800 x 600 or 1024 x 768 is standard but that's not always true. Viewers in niche markets may still use 640 x 480. Ask your programmers or IT about the lowest supported resolution.

Resizing a movie is easy - change the size in the Movie Size tab on the Movie Properties dialog box. But this doesn't resize objects like callouts. You have to change them manually. This is easy but tedious, and is an incentive toward getting the movie's size right the first time.

Tip – If you record a movie, resize it, and create Flash output, the frames may look smeared. To avoid this, get the size right when you first record the movie

Back up a movie before resizing it. If a resize isn't right, just go back to the original.

1. Open the movie.

2. Select **Movie > Properties** OR click the Movie Properties icon on the Frame toolbar.

   The Movie Properties dialog box opens.

3. Select the Movie Size tab.

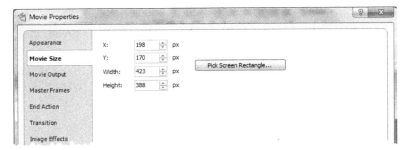

The Movie Size tab lets you set the coordinates of the upper left corner of the window and the height and width from that corner.

- **X/Y** – The coordinates of the upper left corner of the window.

- **Width/Height** – The window width and height from the upper left corner.

- **Pick Screen Rectangle** – To display a red-bordered selection box for resizing the window visually. At the bottom, you'll see the box width and height.

Click and drag a side or corner grab handle to resize the box. (The width and height numbers change accordingly.) Click and drag the four-way arrow in the center text box to move the entire box.

4. Click **OK**.

Object Anchors

When you resize a movie, frame objects retain their position on the overall screen, which can differ from the frame. This sounds logical but can cause trouble. For example, if you add a callout box at the right edge of a frame, then resize the movie, the box will still be at the edge but may now extend off the side of the frame. What you want to do is keep the position of the object relative to the edge of the frame by retaining that distance. In other words, the object should always be ¼" from the edge of the frame no matter the size of the frame.

Object anchors do that. To use them, just select the object and specify the frame edges to which to anchor it. The object will then always stay at the same distance from those edges.

Note – This may not always work *effectively* because different anchored objects may interfere with each other.

Using Object Anchors

1. Open the frame containing the object to anchor and click on the object.

2. Select **View > Show Anchor Arrows**.

   Gray arrows display on each side of the object, circled in the example below, showing the edges of the frame to which you can anchor the object.

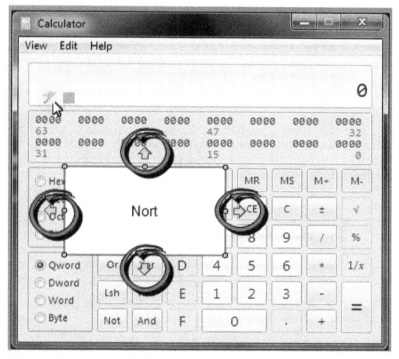

3. Click on the arrows for the edges to which you want to anchor the object.

   The arrow changes color to orange. After you resize and build the movie output, you'll see that the object has remained in the same relative position as opposed to shifting its position.

8 Generating Output

You'll often preview a movie while you develop it, but ultimately you have to generate the finished output for you and reviewers to see the real thing, and to distribute to the viewers.

Generating finished output is the last step in a project but not a final one. If you see something that needs to be changed, re-open the project, make the change, and re-generate the output.

You can generate the output in two forms – an individual finished product or as the output of one or more targets.

An individual finished product is just that – a single output from a single movie or collection. If all you need is one movie or group of movies, all you need is an individual finished product. However, if you need several versions of the same movie, you'll create and use targets instead. A target is an instance, or version, of an output. For example...

Let's say you create a movie that shows how to perform task A for client 1. You're then asked to create what is essentially the same movie but for client 2. You *could* create and maintain two movies that were almost identical, but that would be inefficient. Instead, you can create one movie and then, by using variables and conditions, make Mimic create two outputs, or versions, of the movie, both showing task A but one for client 1 and one for client 2. Each output – for client 1 and client 2 – are targets. The same holds true if you want to create SWF and Silverlight versions of the same movie. The SWF and Silverlight versions are targets. You can further focus your outputs by creating "mixed" targets, such as SWF and Silverlight versions for clients 1 and 2. And so on...

This chapter starts by explaining how to generate a single out-put, and discusses targets at the end of the chapter.

There are four steps to building the finished output.

1.   Decide which format your users need.

2.   Specify the output settings.

3.   Generate the output. This builds the output locally, in the Output folder under the project folder you created when you first saved the project.

4.   Deliver the finished movie to your viewers. You can copy and distribute the output files, or publish them directly to the desired target.

Selecting the Output Format

Mimic offers six output formats. They're summarized below. For more details, see "About Movie Output Formats" in the Mimic help.

Mimic Movie Format (MMF)

MMF is a proprietary format from MadCap designed to run on the desktop rather than from a server. Requires the standalone MadCap Movie Viewer on the viewer's PC.

Consider using this format if you:

- Need higher compression than Flash format offers.

- Need to modify the output files in an XML editor.

- Need to run the movies locally.

- Can download the viewer to the local PC.

Potential stumbling blocks include:

- Inability to run from a server.

- Need to have the viewer on the users' PC. This prevents use of MMF in "zero-footprint"/"thin client" environments where applications can't be downloaded.

- Pre-defined interface that can't be customized.

Microsoft Silverlight

Silverlight resembles Flash – cross-platform and cross-browser capable. It can also be viewed directly in a browser, so it can be viewed on almost any web-ready PC. Silverlight is a proprietary format from Microsoft.

Consider using this format if you:

- You need to run the movies locally and from a server.

- Viewers don't have the Flash player and can't download it to their PCs.

Potential stumbling blocks include:

- The need for a server administrator to configure the MIME types on the server if you plan to run Silverlight moves from the server. It's not difficult – see "Setting the MIME Type on a Server for

Silverlight" in the Mimic help – but you may have to convince the administrator of the benefit of using Silverlight in place of Flash.

Adobe Flash

Flash is a widely used output format for from Adobe. This is due partly to Flash's flexibility – it will run on almost any platform and under almost any browser – and partly to Flash's ubiquity. Almost any web-ready PC is enabled for Flash, which simplifies setup.

Viewers must have the Flash Player on their PCs in order to view a Flash movie, rarely a problem because the player *is* so common. But some viewers may not have the player and not be allowed to install it.

Consider using this format if you:

- Need Flash-based movies.

- Have viewers who download the Flash Player to their PCs.

- Need to customize the toolbar.

- Need to run the movies locally and from a server.

Potential stumbling blocks include:

- Viewers who don't have the player and who are behind a firewall that blocks them from downloading it will not be able to view the movies.

- If you want to create movies to run on the iPhone, iPad, or other Apple mobile devices, note that Apple has prohibited the use of Flash on such devices as of late 2011.

- The finished file size is larger than the corresponding MadCap Movie Player file size.

Adobe AIR

AIR (Adobe Integrated Runtime) is a hybrid of a web-based format and a desktop format. It encapsulates all the movie files into one distributable file that runs on the viewers' PCs but can be upgraded via the web or from a server. In theory, this is the best of both worlds – local operation for speed and freedom from internet connection and traffic load problems and web-sensitivity for downloads.

Consider using this format if you:

- Want to generate the movies in one file for ease of distribution.

- Need movies that adhere to the AIR standard.
- Need movies that can be updated over the web.
- Need to customize the toolbar.

Potential stumbling blocks include:

- The need to install the Java Runtime Environment (JRE) on your development PC in order to generate the output. In high-security environments, IT may have to do this.
- The need to install AIR on your development PC and on viewers' PCs in order to view the output. In high-security environments, IT may have to do this.
- Possible or perceived security problems in creating and running a format that can harbor viruses and access local PC features. Adobe offers a digital certificate feature to deal with this, but talk to your IT or network manager before picking this option.

PDF

Adobe's PDF (Portable Document Format) is proprietary but has existed for so long as to be a de facto standard for "print-oriented" output.

Consider using this format if you:

- Want to generate the movies in a single file for easy distribution to multiple platforms.
- Want to generate the movies to be printed or look like hard-copy on the screen and be viewable through a browser or the PDF reader.

Potential stumbling blocks include:

- None per se.

XPS

Microsoft's XPS (XML Paper Specification) is similar to and competes with PDF.

Consider using this format if you:

- Work in a Microsoft-oriented shop.
- Want to generate the movies in one file for ease of distribution to multiple platforms.

- Want to generate the movies either to be printed or to look like hard-copy on the screen, and to be viewable through a browser.

- Faster compilation than PDF, though this may not be significant.

Potential stumbling blocks include:

- XPS is less common and thus less familiar than PDF.

Which Output Format to Use

You'll probably use the one most suitable format, but you're not limited to one format. You can change formats for a movie if you want to test different options, or create multiple targets for a movie and use different output formats in the different targets.

Scenarios for Output Types

Let's review some scenarios that require different formats.

#1: Training for a Windows Desktop Application

Your company sells electronic medical record software that runs locally on XP PCs. The software is installed from CD or by download from your company web site, and there are no plans to make it server-based. The application is largely clerical, so the users are not highly skilled with PCs and there's a lot of turnover. However, most users have home PCs that they use to surf the web. You want to add tutorials to get users up to speed on the application and cut down calls to technical support.

What are your options?

MadCap Movie or Flash will work since each one will run locally. The MadCap Movie format is more efficient technically, but viewers may prefer Flash since it looks like what they might see on the web.

#2: Training for a Web-Based Application

Recast scenario #1. The company moved the application to the web and wants as little as possible installed on users' PCs. Everything else is the same – the application is clerical and there's lot of turnover, but most users have home PCs that they use to surf the web. You want to add tutorials to help users learn the application and reduce support calls.

What are your options?

You could use Flash, AIR, or Silverlight because they will run from a server as well as locally on the users' PCs. Plus Flash resembles what they might see on the web. AIR or Silverlight may also, but these two formats are newer than Flash and less common.

Specifying the Output Settings

The settings are similar for all the outputs. Mimic automatically changes the available settings, depending on which output you select.

1. Open a movie.

2. Select **Movie > Properties** OR click the Movie Properties icon on the Frame toolbar.

   The Movie Properties dialog box opens.

3. Select the Movie Output tab.

   Note – This tab displays if you open the Movie Properties dialog box from a movie. If you're creating a collection, specify the settings on the Options tab of the Collection Editor instead.

4. Select the desired options from the Movie Output tab.

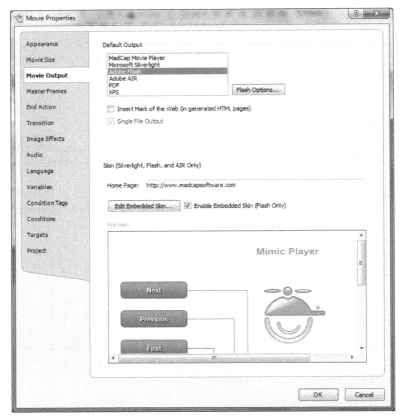

The Movie Output tab lets you specify the final output settings for the movie.

- **Default Output** – The desired output format. Each option, except the MadCap Movie Player, can be customized to varying degrees. The options are straightforward, except for the digital certificate and installer settings for AIR. See your IT manager for details for your company.

- **Insert Mark of... Web** – For Silverlight, Flash, or AIR. Hides the "blocked content" warning that displays if you open a local HTML file. You only need this option if the movie will run on users' local PCs rather than on a web server.

- **Single File Output** – For MadCap Movie Player. Creates one file that contains the entire movie output. Deselect this option to create multiple output files for the movie. One file means easier distribution; multiple files mean more files to distribute but the files are small and load quickly.

- **Home Page** – For Silverlight, Flash, or AIR. Sets the URL for a home page that viewers can access by clicking a Home icon on the toolbar. (You define the Home icon through the Skin Editor.)

- **Edit Skin** – For Silverlight, Flash, or AIR. Displays the Skin Editor where you can create or modify a skin.

5. Click **OK**.

Building the Output

Once you define the output settings, you can create the output any time. You're generating the output locally, typically on your C: drive. The process is basically the same for any of the formats.

1. Open a movie.

2. Select **Movie > Build** OR click the Build the Active Movie/ Collection icon on the standard toolbar.

   The Build Progress dialog box opens.

3. When the build ends, click Yes if a message asks if you want to view the output.

   The movie displays in the viewing mechanism for that output format – MadCap Movie Player, your browser, etc.

Distributing the Finished Output

There are two ways to distribute the output to your users.

- Move the files manually.

- Use Mimic's Publish feature.

Move the Files Manually

In this approach, you find the required files in the appropriate subfolder under the project's Output folder and copy them to whatever distribution medium you want to use, such as a CD, DVD, email attachment, etc.

What files do you need to distribute?

- **MadCap Movie format** – For a movie, the mcmovie folder and its contents, and create a link to the mcmovie file. For a collection, the mcmoviesysf folder and create a link to the mcmoviesys file.

- **Adobe Flash format** – For a movie, the mcmvf folder and its contents, and create a link to the HTM file. For a collection, the mcmvf folder and its contents, and create a link to the HTM file for the movie to be played first.

- **Adobe AIR format** – For a movie, the one file in the adobeair folder. For a collection, the same.

- **Microsoft Silverlight format** – For a movie, the mcmvf folder and its contents, and create a link to the HTM file. For a collection, the mcmvf folder and its contents, and create a link to the HTM file for the movie to be played first in that movie's subfolder under the mcmvf folder.

Publish the Files

Mimic's "publish" feature can automatically move the movie files to the desired delivery point, usually a server or network drive, if you have the publishing rights. The publish feature is optional, but it can take some of the work off your hands.

To output to Adobe Flash:

1. Open a movie.
2. Select **Movie > Publish** or **Collection > Publish**.

   The Publish dialog box opens.

Select from or specify these options:

- **Type** – Select FTP to publish to a server, or File System to publish to a network drive or locally.

- **Host Name** – The server to which to publish the output. Only available if you select FTP for the Type.

- **Directory** – Select a directory from the dropdown or click the Browse button to find the publishing target directory. You can also create a target directory from this field.

- **Anonymous Login** – To publish to a server without entering a user name and password. (The network administrator may not allow this.) Only available if you select FTP for the Type.

- **Login Credentials** – To enter a user name and password now, rather than waiting for the server to request it. Only available if you select FTP for the Type and enter a host name.

- **Port** – The port to use to connect to the server, if you select FTP for the Type. Ask your network administrator.

- **Optional "View" URL** – To enter an optional http address through which to view the movie.

- **Upload Only Changed Files** – To publish only the files that changed since the last time you published the movie.

- **Remove Stale Files** – To remove files published to the destination in a previous pass but no longer needed.

3. Click the Start Publishing button.

   The Build Progress dialog box opens.

4. When the publishing ends, you can view a log of the published files.

5. Run or link to the starter file to run the movie or collection.

Targets

There may be times when you need multiple versions of one movie, each tailored slightly for individual clients, product versions, output formats, etc. The problem is that each version is an individual movie project that's easy to create but difficult to maintain. Targets solve this problem.

A target is a collection of output options. For example, you might define a target called "Flash – Eastern Sales Region" that uses the Flash output format and excludes any material not related to the eastern sales region. You could define another target called "Flash – Western Sales Region" that uses Flash output format and excludes any material not related to the western sales region. And so on. In effect, a target is a "filter" that extracts specific material from a project and applies specific settings to generate a specific output. You can define as many targets as you need for a movie project.

Creating a Target

To create a target:

1. Open the Movie project for which you want to define a target.

2. Select **Movie > Properties**.

   The Movie Properties dialog box opens.

3. Select the Targets tab.

   The Targets screen displays.

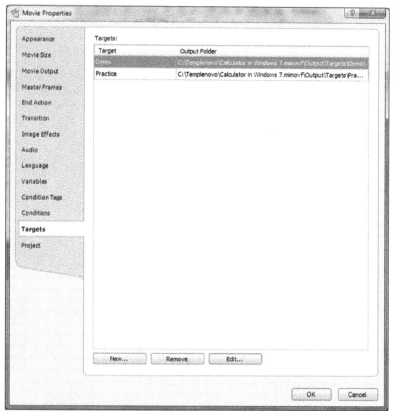

The Targets screen offers these options:

- **New** – To define a new target.

- **Remove** – To delete an existing target.

- **Edit** – To edit an existing target.

4. Click the New button.

   The New Target dialog box opens.

5. Select the General tab.

The General tab has one field, Title – the target's title for use in development. Give targets clearly descriptive names "Flash for Eastern Sales Region" rather than something vague like "East."

5. Click the Movie Output tab.

The Movie Output dialog box opens.

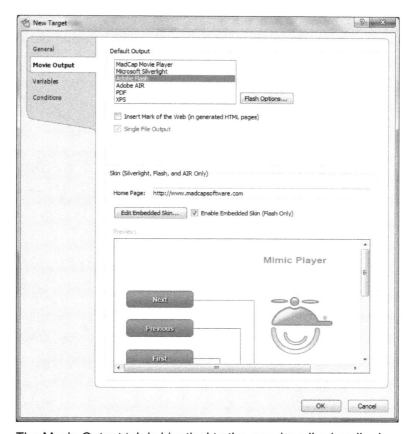

The Movie Output tab is identical to the one described earlier in this chapter for specifying output settings. Make the appropriate settings for the target.

6.   Click the Variables tab.

The Variables dialog box opens.

The Variables screen lists all variables and their values. It lets you change a variable's value *for this target*. For example, let's say you previously created a variable called Region and set its definition, or value, to Western. If you're defining this new target for the eastern sales region, you could change the Region variable's value to Eastern.

7. Click the Conditions tab.

The Conditions dialog box opens.

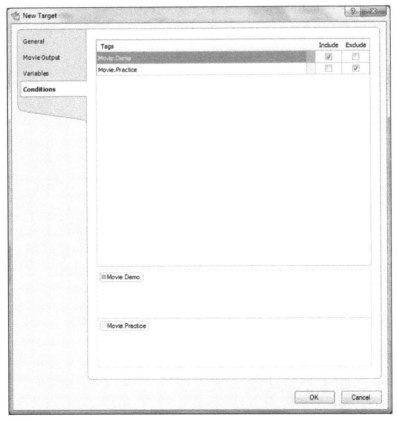

The Conditions screen lets you specify what conditions to use for *this* target. The top part of the screen lists all existing conditions. Specify the material to include in or exclude by clicking the appropriate check boxes. To keep tabs on the conditions you've applied, see the fields at the bottom of the screen. In the screen above, for example, you're including all material conditionalized as Demo but not specifically excluding any other material.

Whether you include or exclude material for a target depends on your goals for the target and the conditions you applied to the material earlier, so it's important to plan the conditions you need before creating and applying the conditional tags. For example, you might decide that you want to use all of the type A material but none of the type B material. In that case, you could simply select the Exclude option for the type B-conditionalized material. That way, the type A material, being unselected, will be used by default in the output but the type B material, being selected for exclusion, will not. See the discussion of conditionality in the Advanced Features chapter for some more conceptual discussion about the creation and use of conditions.

8. Click **OK**.

   You return to the Movie Properties tab.

9. Click **OK**.

   You return to the movie.

Building Targets

If you defined one or more targets for a Mimic movie, you can generate all the targets at once or a subset. To generate all the targets at once, simply select the regular build option. If you only want to generate one target or a few, you can do so instead by selecting from a list of available targets that you can see on the standard toolbar.

1. Open a movie.

2. Click the Build Targets button near the right-hand end of the Standard toolbar.

   The Build Targets dialog box opens.

3. Click in the check box for each target that you want to compile, then click the Build button.

    Mimic builds the specified targets and puts their output files in whatever folder you specified, or the default Output folder. You can then select and distribute those files like any other output.

9 Frame Interactivity Features

Chapter 5 discussed basic annotation features like callouts and highlight boxes. This chapter discusses features that let you add interactivity to your movies.

Demonstrations vs. Simulations

You can use Mimic to create different kinds of movies, but they're often software training in the form of demonstrations or simulations.

- Demonstrations typically show how to perform a task. They use callouts, highlight boxes, and other features to explain what's happening on the screen but they're passive. Viewers watch, perhaps listen to narration on some screens, but there's little or no interaction with the movie. So demonstrations are a good way to present tasks and concepts but offer little reinforcement.

- Simulations are the opposite. By adding interactivity to a movie, you can almost make viewers think they're using the real software. For example, you can use a "click box" to simulate a menu click in the real software. The movie stops until the viewer "clicks" that menu item, at which point the movie continues, like the real software.

Tip – You may find it useful to create two versions of the same movie – a demonstration that viewers watch to see how to perform a task and a simulation where they "perform" that task in order to test their retention.

Interactivity Features

Mimic's features let you create interactivity in ways that go far beyond what we'll discuss here. However, three features lend themselves particularly well to interactivity:

- Buttons and links – To create on-screen buttons that viewers can click to advance to the next slide in a movie, jump to a URL, etc.

- Click boxes – To create screen "hot spots" and define what happens if a viewer clicks on them. They're often used to simulate menu clicks.

- User input boxes – To create screen "hot spots" for simulated text entry.

How might you use these features in a movie?

Let's say that a frame has so much material in callouts and rollovers that it's hard to decide how long to display it to give viewers time to read and absorb everything. So you stop the automatic movie advance and add a button that moves to the next frame only when viewers click on it.

The next frame might contain a screen on which viewers must make a menu selection. This is a simulation, so the movie stops and waits for the viewer to click. No click, no action.

The next frame might show a dialog box containing a text field in which the viewer must make an entry. This is a simulation so, again, the movie stops, waits for the viewer to type the entry, verifies it, and then moves on. No entry, no action.

The simulation features are more complex than the basic annotation features but still straightforward. A button is just an area of the screen made to look like a button, with an action defined to take place if viewers click on it. The complexity comes from two other factors.

- Each feature has many options. You'll want to use a sub-set of them so as not to visually saturate the viewers.

- These features control viewers' paths through a movie. It's important to not get viewers lost or confused.

Create a Simulation

You create simulations like demonstrations, as described in chapter 4. The difference is in the Mimic features you use; especially turning off the Add Callouts and Record Cursor Movements options since simulations won't have callouts or automatic mouse movement.

Buttons

Buttons can be very useful. For example, let's say that a particular frame contains a lot of information, making it hard to decide how long to display the frame so that users have the time to read and absorb the information. Rather than pick a duration that won't satisfy anyone, simply pause the movie to let viewers read at their own pace. A "Click to continue" button takes them to the next frame.

Note – To pause at a frame, open the frame, select **Frame > Properties**, click the Transition tab, select the Pause Movie… option, and click **OK**. This turns off the automatic frame advance so viewers must click on the button to go to the next frame. You *can* create a button but not pause the movie, in which case the movie will go to the next frame whether or not the viewer clicks the button. This can be confusing since the simulation will work even if the viewer does nothing.

For another example, say you create a movie describing a WorldWide Web Consortium (W3C) feature in your application, so you add a button labeled W3C that jumps viewers to the WorldWide Web Consortium site.

Creating Buttons

1. Display the frame on which to add the button.

2. Click the Button Mode icon   on the Frames toolbar, or click the icon's pulldown and select **Button Mode**.

   The pointer changes to a small cross-hair.

3. Click in the frame roughly where the button should go, hold the left mouse button down, and drag out the button's rectangle shape. Don't worry if the size or position aren't right; you can change them at any time.

   The result is a button with the default label "Click Me" and a yellow circle icon with a flag. This icon means you have not defined the button action.

   You can use the grab handles on the button corners and sides to resize the button, but that's pointless until you see how long the caption is and thus how big the actual button must be.

   You can also click inside the button and drag to move it.

4. To set the button properties, double click on the button. The Button Properties dialog box opens. Some of the tabs, like Time Span and Shadow, are either similar to or identical to other instances of those tabs.

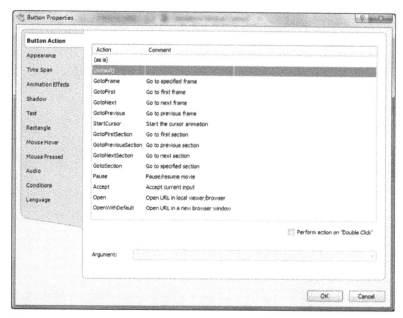

The Button Action tab lets you specify the action to perform when the viewer clicks on the button. The options are self-explanatory.

Depending on the option you pick, you may have to add more information in the Argument field. You can also require a double-click on the button by selecting the Perform Action on "Double Click" option.

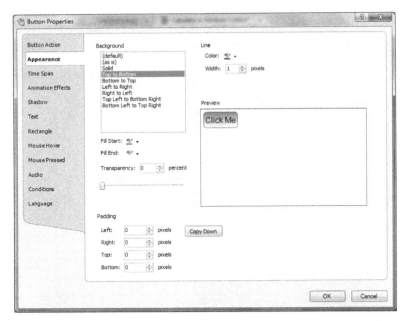

The Appearance tab lets you set the button's color and border values:

- **Background** — To set the button's background color as solid or as a gradient in different directions.

- **Fill Start/Fill End** — To set the starting and ending colors if you use a color gradient for the background.

- **Transparency** — To set the degree of transparency or opacity of the background colors.

- **Padding** – To control the blank space between the edges of the button and the text.

- **Copy Down** – To copy the setting in the first (Left) Padding field to the other three Padding fields.

- **Color** – To set the color of the button's border.

- **Width** – To set the width of the button's border.

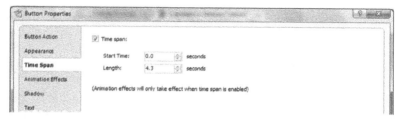

The Time Span tab lets you set the starting time and duration. You can also change these settings by using the timeline.

- **Start Time** — The time at which to start displaying the button.

- **Length** — The amount of time to display the button.

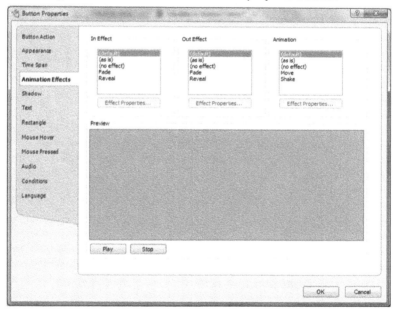

The Animation Effects tab lets you set animation effects that control how the button appears and disappears, such as through a fade in and out or a "reveal", and any animation effects to play while the button displays.

- **In Effect** — The effect as the button opens. This can be a fade in, a reveal (the button slides in), the default (no effect unless you added the button to the palette and specified an effect there), as is, or no effect.

143

- **Out Effect** — The effect as the button closes. Same options as In Effect.

    Each option's Effect Properties button opens a dialog box where you can set the effect's direction and duration.

- **Animation** — The effect while the button displays. You can select from a move (the box moves along a path defined by clicking on the box, clicking the Trajectory Mode icon on the Frame toolbar, and dragging the box to its end point), a shake (the box shakes up and/or down for a specified duration), the default (no effect unless you added the box to the palette and specified an effect there), as is, or no effect.

    The Effect Properties button opens a dialog box where you can set the effect's direction and duration.

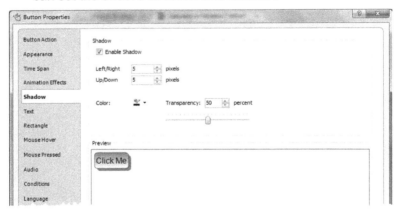

The Shadow tab lets you add a shadow to the button:

- **Enable Shadow** — To turn on the shadow effect.

- **Left/Right** — To set the shadow's horizontal offset from the button.

- **Up/Down** — To set the shadow's vertical offset from the button.

- **Color** – To set the shadow's color.

- **Transparency** – To set the shadow's transparency.

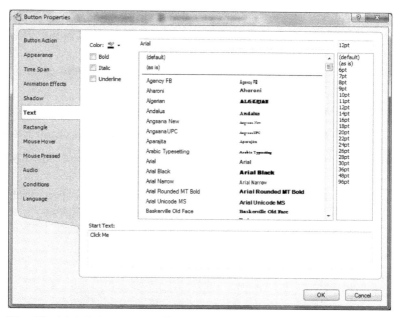

The Text tab lets you specify the font attributes for the button label. All the options on this tab should be self-explanatory.

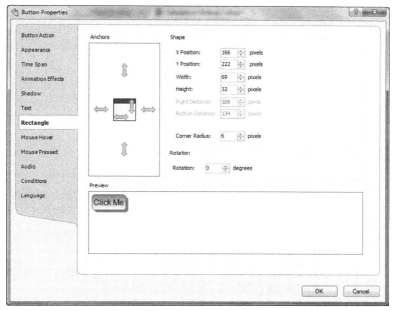

The Rectangle tab lets you set the button's size and position. You can also change the size by modifying the button itself rather than on this tab.

- **Shape – X Position/Y Position** — To set the co-ordinates of the upper left corner of the button.

- **Width** — To set the button width from the upper left corner.

- **Height** — To set the button height from the upper left corner.

- **Corner Radius** – To set the corner curvature. The lower the number, the squarer. The higher, the rounder.

- **Rotation** – To set the button rotation. A positive number is clockwise rotation, negative is counter-clockwise.

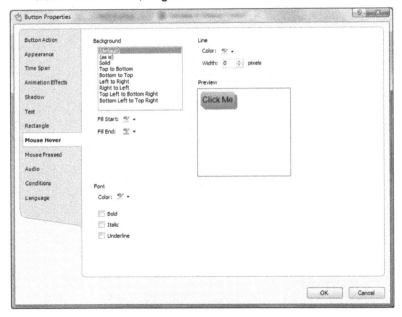

The Mouse Hover tab lets you set the button color, border, and text values when the viewer hovers the mouse pointer over it:

- **Background** — To set the button's background color as solid or as a gradient in different directions.

- **Fill Start/Fill End** — To set the starting and ending colors if you use a gradient for the background.

- **Color** – To set the color of the button's label.

- **Bold/Italic/Underline** – To set those text enhancement properties for the button's label.

- **Color** – To set the color of the button's border.

- **Width** – To set the thickness of the button's border.

The Mouse Pressed tab has the same options for setting the button color, border, and text values when viewers click on it.

The Audio tab lets you add audio to a button by importing an existing audio clip or recording a new one. It's the same as the Audio tab described in the Basic Frame Annotation chapter.

The Conditions tab lets you set conditions to the button. It's the same as the Conditions tab discussed in the Basic Frame Annotation chapter.

The Language tab lets you set the spell-check language for the button. It's the same as the Language tab described in the Basic Frame Annotation chapter.

2. When you finish making the settings, click **OK**.

3. Select **Frame > Properties**, click the Transition tab, select the Pause Movie... option, and click **OK**. This turns off the automatic frame advance so that viewers must click on the button in order to go to the next frame.

Click Boxes

Click boxes let you mark an area of a frame as "clickable," and define what happens when viewers click on it. This is similar to a button, except that a button *looks like* a button but a click box is just a hot spot with no inherent look of its own. Its sole purpose is to simulate clickability.

You might place a click box on top of a menu item on a screen shot in the movie and specify that when viewers click on it, the movie will go to the next frame where viewers see a sub-menu. It looks like the real thing but it's just a simulation.

Note – If you use a click box like this, turn off the frame advance for that screen to make it look as if it's the "clicking" that goes to the next frame. Otherwise, the movie advances whether the viewer clicks or not, ruining the effect. To turn off automatic advance, select the Pause Movie at End of Frame option on the Transition tab of the Frame Properties dialog box.

Creating Click Boxes

A click box is just a rectangle, circle, or polygon, like a highlight box and with the same features. So if you've created highlight boxes, you know how to create click boxes. But unlike a highlight box, you don't want the click box to be shown on top of the item whose "click" you're simulating since that would ruin the effect. So the only tabs you should use for a click box are Appearance, to make it invisible, and Action, to specify what happens when the viewer clicks on it.

The instructions below explain how to create a rectangular click box. To create an oval or polygonal one, use the Appearance and Action tabs on the Oval Properties or Polygon Properties dialog boxes.

Rectangular Click Box:

1. Display the frame on which to add a click box.

2. Click the Rectangle Mode icon ⊞ on the Frame Editor toolbar.

   The pointer changes to a small cross-hair.

3. Draw a tightly-fitting box around the object to be "click-boxed."

   Notice the grab handles on the corners and sides of the click box. Click on and drag any of the grab handles to resize or move the box.

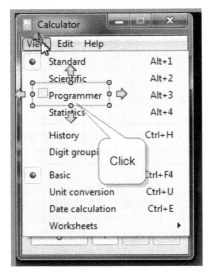

4. To set the click box's properties, double click it to open the Rectangle, Oval, or Polygon Properties dialog box. You'll probably use just the Appearance and Action tabs.

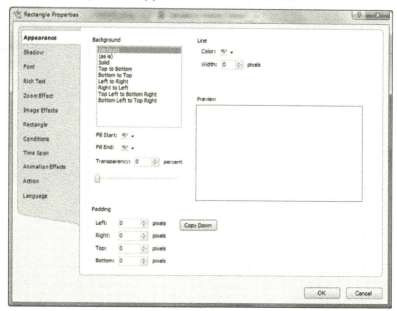

The Appearance tab lets you set the click box's color and border values.

Note – To make a click box invisible, set the Width to 0. Ignore the other settings.

- **Background** — To set the callout's background color as solid or as a gradient in different directions.

- **Fill Start/Fill End** — To set the starting and ending colors if you use a color gradient for the background.

- **Transparency** — To set the degree of transparency of the background colors.

- **Padding** – To set the amount of blank space between the edges of the callout box and the text.

- **Color** – To set the color of the box's border.

- **Width** – To set the width of the box's border.

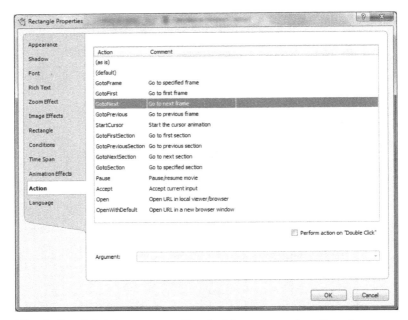

The Action tab lets you specify what happens when the viewer clicks on the click box. The options are self-explanatory.

5. When you finish, click **OK**.

6. Select **Frame > Properties**, click the Transition tab, select the Pause Movie… option, and click **OK**. This turns off the automatic frame advance; viewers must click on the button to go to the next frame.

Typing Boxes and Input Boxes

Mimic can simulate text entry on a frame in two ways – entered by Mimic automatically or by the viewers themselves.

- **Typing box** – Defines an area of the screen to contain text that Mimic enters. For example, you might create a frame containing a field that calls for an entry and let viewers watch Mimic enter it for them.

  You *can* use a typing box and input box to give users the option of watching Mimic make the entry or making it themselves – "show me" vs. "let me try it." But this complicates the movie's flow because you'll have to define two paths for viewers to follow. For example, let's say slide 1 calls for an entry in a simulated field and lets viewers make it themselves or let Mimic do it. No matter who makes the entry, the movie goes on. This means that the movie diverges into two paths at slide 1 and comes back into one path a few slides later.

- **Input box** – Defines an area of the screen for text the *viewer* must enter. For example, a frame can show a dialog box field in which viewers must type a file name or a "quiz" frame where they must type an answer to a question. You can customize this by defining right answer(s), specifying how many attempts viewers get, feedback, and the action to take for right or wrong answers.

Input boxes can cause three problems, so use them carefully.

- Bad entries – Viewers can mistype an entry and not see the error, so show the right answer in the failure feedback.

- Bad entries that *look* OK – Viewers may use different names for the same thing, such as sub, hoagie, hero, torpedo, etc. The risk is that viewers will type what *they* think is the right entry, only to have it marked wrong because it's not in *your* list of right answers. Solicit input from viewers to be sure you include every possible right answer in the list of answers.

- Visual overkill – The Input Box Properties dialog box lets you set fill and border colors, box border width, animation effects, etc. These features are useful if you're creating an input box meant to be seen as an input box. However, if you're creating an input box meant to simulate a field entry, these enhancements will clash visually with the field borders.

Creating Typing Boxes

A typing box is a text box in which Mimic inserts the text for the viewer.

1. Display the frame on which to add the typing box.

2. Click the Button Mode icon ⌐ ▾ pulldown on the Frame Editor toolbar and select Typing Box Mode.

   The pointer changes to a small crosshair.

3. Click in the upper left corner of the area in which to add the typing box, hold the left mouse button down, and drag out the box. Don't worry if the size or position aren't right; you can adjust

them at any time.

Note the grab handles on the corners and sides of the box.

4. Click on and drag any of the grab handles to resize the box. Click in and drag the box to move it.

5. To set the box's properties, double click it. The Typing Box Properties dialog box opens.

Most Typing Box properties are identical to other tabs described earlier in this book, so this section looks at the one tab peculiar to typing boxes – the Typing Box tab.

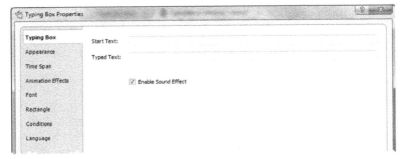

The Typing Box tab lets you specify text to display in the typing box when it opens, and the text to automatically insert.

- **Start Text** — Any optional text to display in the box when the frame containing the box displays.

- **Typed Text** — The text to automatically enter in the box.

- **Enable Sound Effect** — To add a key-click sound for the text being automatically entered in the box.

6. When you finish, click **OK**.

Creating Input Boxes

An input box is a text box in which the viewer types the text.

1. Display the frame on which to add the input box.

2. Click the Button Mode icon pulldown on the Frame Editor toolbar and select Input Box Mode.

The pointer changes to a small cross-hair.

3. Click near the upper left corner of the area in which to add the input box, hold the left mouse button down, and drag out the box. Don't worry if the size or position aren't right; you can adjust them at any time.

The yellow circle and flag icon means that you have not yet defined the input box's action.

Note the grab handles on the corners and sides of the typing box.

4. Click on and drag any of the grab handles to resize the box. Click in and drag the box to move it.

5. To set the input box's properties, double click it. The Input Box Properties dialog box opens.

Most Input Box properties are identical to tabs described earlier in this book, so this section looks at those tabs peculiar to input boxes, the Input Box, Success Action, Failure Action, and Appearance tabs.

The Input Box tab lets you specify correct entries, and the number of tries that a viewer has to get it right.

- **Correct Entry** — To specify correct answers. To add multiple right answers, type each one on a separate line. The answers are not case-sensitive.

- **Allow user** — The number of attempts a viewer gets to type the right answer. To set a specific number, deselect Infinite Attempts and set a number in the Attempts field.

  If you leave the number set to Infinite, there is no failure feedback since the viewer can never get the answer wrong. If you specify any other number, the Failure feedback box displays after the last wrong answer.

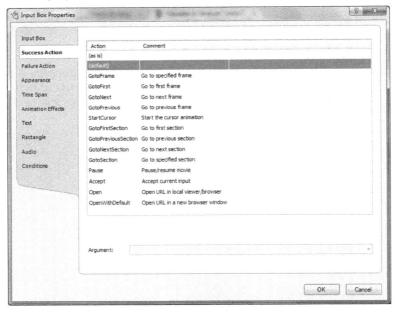

The Success Action tab lets you specify an action to per-form after a viewer enters a right answer. Select the action and type or select the appropriate settings in the Argument field. The actions are the same as those in other Action tabs.

The Failure Action tab has the same options but is only available if you change the number of attempts, defined on the Input Box tab, from Infinite to a specific number.

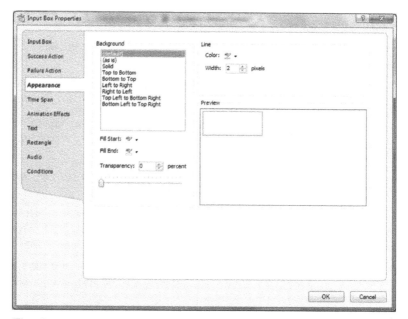

The Appearance tab lets you specify the input box's color and border settings:

- **Background** — To set the box's background color as solid or a gradient in different directions.

- **Fill Start/Fill End** — To set the starting and ending colors if you use a gradient for the background.

- **Transparency** — To set the degree of transparency of the background colors.

- **Color** – To set the color of the box's border.

- **Width** – To set the width of the box's border.

6. When you finish, click **OK**.

7. Select **Frame > Properties**, click the Transition tab, select the Pause Movie... option, and click **OK**. This turns off the automatic frame advance, forcing viewers to make an entry to go to the next frame.

Adding Feedback to Input Boxes

You can attach three types of feedback to an input box in order to help or guide viewers.

- **Success** – A message to show if viewers type the right answer. The message should be short and professional – "Good job!"

- **Failure** – A message to show if viewers type the wrong answer. The message should be friendly and helpful – "Please try again" rather than "No, you dope!"

- **Hint** – A message to show if viewers move the pointer over the input box – "Please type the answer here".

This is similar to what you'd say if you were showing someone how to do a task. "That's it" if they get it right, "No, try again" if they get it wrong, and "That's it – type the answer there" if they mouse over the input box.

The three types of feedback use the same dialog boxes and tabs, with one exception. The steps below describe how to create a success feedback box.

To create a feedback caption box:

1. Click on the input box to which to add the feedback box.

2. Click the Button Mode icon ![icon] pulldown on the Frame Editor toolbar and select Input Success/Failure/Hint Caption Mode.

   The pointer changes to a small cross-hair.

3. Click in the upper left corner of the area in which to add the feedback caption box, hold the left mouse button down, and drag out the box which displays the appropriate "Enter... text here" prompt. Don't worry if the size or position aren't right; you can adjust them at any time.

   Place feedback boxes close to the input box they refer to. If the boxes are too far away, viewers may literally not notice them.

   Note the grab handles on the corners and sides of the feedback box.

4. Click on and drag any of the grab handles to resize the box. Click in and drag the box to move it.

5. To set the box's properties, double click it. The Success, Failure, or Hint Caption Properties dialog box opens.

   These tabs are identical to those for callout boxes, except for the Time Span tab which lets you set the box's duration. (You can also change this setting by using the timeline.) This tab isn't available for a Hint since a Hint displays as long as the viewer hovers the pointer over the input box

   Note – This Time Span tab doesn't have the Start Time option since the feedback displays after a viewer types an answer or hovers the mouse over the input box, rather than after some time period.

6. When you finish, click **OK**.

10 Advanced Features

This chapter presents a mix of features that let you extend the power of your movies, integrate them into other movies, tie them to Flare to create integrated help systems, and more.

Adding Audio

When used well, audio can increase a movie's effectiveness and usability. Audio is often used to add voice narration to frames in order to explain them audibly in addition to text in a callout. But you can also add audio to frame objects, such as attaching a "ping" to a callout, or add audio in the form of background music to an entire movie. You can import existing audio into a movie or record your own voice narration.

Notes and Suggestions About Adding Audio

Adding audio is easy mechanically. The problems lie in the legal issues of using existing audio files, especially music, and doing your own voiceovers if you don't have a trained voice.

With regard to adding sound effects, particularly music:

- For sound effects or music, first try the clips that ship with Mimic, in the Program Files\MadCap Software\ MadCap Mimic V6\ Mimic.app\Resources\Sounds\ MoviePlayer folder. The clips include noises, music, and effects like office background sounds. The clips are free, without copyright restriction, but generic.

- For more choices, search online for "royalty-free music". Be sure any clips you find that way are royalty-free for commercial use, not just personal use, and check to see if there are any time limits. As with the Mimic clip library, royalty-free clips are generic.

- If you really need custom music, hire a composer.

Some Points About Recording Voice Narrations

Starting with the issue of who does it:

- If possible, hire a professional. (Local TV news anchors often do this on the side.) They're expensive, but you're more likely to get a polished result with fewer retakes.

- If you can't afford a professional, try to find someone in-house with voice training, like a serious amateur singer.
- If you can't find anyone in-house with voice training, pick *someone* based on these criteria:
  - A geographically neutral accent.
  - A mid-range voice rather than too high or low.
  - No word mispronunciations.

Recording well is hard. Here are some suggestions for planning:

- Record narration for each frame separately. This way, a mistake on one frame won't ruin the timing of the audio before the mistake or require editing and retiming.
- Write a script for each frame to be narrated, even if only for a sentence. Don't wing it.
- Do dry runs through the script to look for words that can make you stumble, like acronyms, and write acronyms phonetically in the script. (For example, DEC and NEC sound identical but are pronounced "deck" and "en-ee-cee.") You may find it helpful to write them that way.
- Breathe. You want to avoid running out of air and having to take a deep breath that the mike will pick up.

Here are suggestions for the recording equipment and facility:

- If possible, use a noise-shielded professional recording facility.
- Don't record in your cubicle or you'll pick up every noise around. Use a conference room with a door you can close and a fan you can turn off. Consider other ambient noises you normally take for granted, like the rumble of a truck entering an attached garage.
- Put a note on the door stating, in big letters, that you're recording and asking people to be quiet as they walk by. Maybe station a co-worker outside the door to shush people.
- If the door has a window, face away from it while you record to avoid distractions.
- Get good equipment. Professional equipment, even for mundane items like cables, is best but expensive. You *can* get headsets with boom mikes for about $20 at Staples that may be all you need. Try one of these headsets first to see if the quality is okay.

- Get a headset with a boom mike. Once you place the mike, you don't have to keep checking where it is as you talk. (The headset also lets you review your audio without disturbing people around you.) Avoid desktop or handheld mikes; the need to constantly see where your mouth is in relation to the mike is distracting.

Adding Audio to Objects

You can add audio to cursors, buttons, and input boxes, such as adding a "ping" sound to a button to grab viewers' attention when it appears, Do this sparingly. The attention-getting aspect will get lost if you overdo it.

1. Double-click on the object to which to add sound.

   The appropriate Properties dialog box opens.

2. Select the Audio tab and make the appropriate settings. The screen below shows the Audio tab from the Button Properties dialog box. All the Audio tabs are the same save for one exception on the Frame Audio tab, covered in the next section.

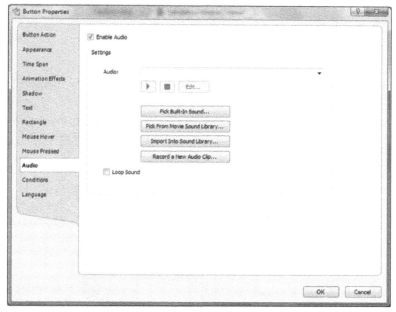

Select the Enable Audio option at the top. Then select from these options:

- **Play, Pause** — To play or pause the selected audio file.

- **Edit** — To open the audio editor for an audio file you recorded. This button is disabled for the audio files that ship with Mimic.

- **Pick Built-In...** — To use one of the audio files that ships with Mimic.

- **Pick From Movie Sound Library** — To re-use a clip that you already imported into the movie and that is now in the sound library. This holds down the movie size since you're simply re-using a clip that's already in the movie.

- **Import Into... Library** — To import an external audio clip in WAV or MP3 format into the movie.

- **Record a New Audio Clip** — Self-explanatory.

- **Loop Sound** — To re-play an audio clip repeatedly until the frame's display time ends. This eliminates the need to find a clip whose duration is the same as that of the frame. (Some of the clips that ship with Mimic offer looped versions, so you don't have to select this option if you use one of those clips.)

3. When you finish, click **OK**.

Adding Audio to Frames

Frame audio is typically voice narration. Adding it is almost identical to adding audio to objects.

If you add voice to frames with callouts, consider whether the audio must be identical to the callout text or can differ from or expand on it. You'll find various opinions about this question and two problems:

- Cognitive overload – Presenting the material as text and audio simultaneously adds flexibility by letting viewers follow their preferred cognitive channel. But it can also complicate retention by overloading viewers as they try to follow those two channels simultaneously. There's a good discussion about this in *e-Learning and the Science of Instruction* by Ruth Colvin Clark and Richard E. Meyer, published in 2003 by Pfeiffer.

- Channel comparison distraction – If you present material as text and audio simultaneously but the channels aren't identical, viewers may get distracted by looking for and trying to resolve differences in the two channels rather than paying attention to the actual content.

You can add audio to frames by importing existing clips, like voice recordings made off-site, or by recording voice directly through Mimic.

To add audio to a frame:

1. Double-click on the frame to which to add sound.

   The Frame Properties dialog box opens.

2. Select the Audio tab and make all required settings. The Frame Audio tab is almost identical to the object Audio tabs except for the addition of the Stop Sound of Previous Frame option.

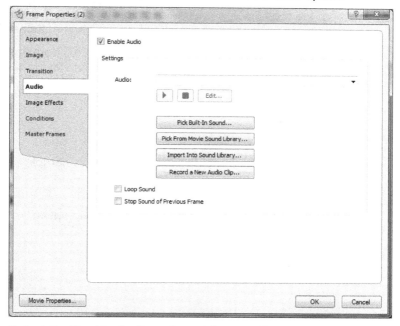

Select the Enable Audio option at the top. Then select from the following options:

- **Play, Pause** — To play or pause the selected audio.

- **Edit** — To open the audio editor for an audio file that you recorded. This button is disabled for the audio files that ship with Mimic.

- **Pick Built-In...** — To use one of the audio files that ships with Mimic.

- **Pick From Movie Sound Library** — To re-use a clip that you already imported into the movie and is now in the sound library. This holds down the movie size since you're re-using a clip already in the movie.

- **Import Into... Library** — To import an external audio clip in WAV or MP3 format into the movie.

- **Record a New Audio Clip** — Self-explanatory.

- **Loop Sound** — To re-play an audio clip repeatedly until the frame's display time ends. This eliminates the need to find a clip whose duration is the same as that of the frame. (Some of the clips that ship with Mimic offer looped versions, so you don't have to select this option if you use one of those clips.)

- **Stop Sound of Previous...** — To stop audio from the previous frame if that audio lasts longer than its frame and thus continues on this new frame.

3. When you finish, click **OK**.

Recording Voice Narration

1. Double-click on the frame to which to add voice narration.

   The Frame Properties dialog box opens.

2. Select the Audio tab and click the Enable Audio option.

3. Click the Record a New Audio Clip button.

   The Record dialog box opens.

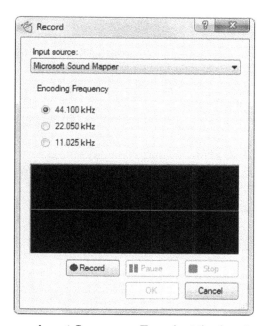

- **Input Source** — To select the input source, typically your mike. You can use the default.

- **Encoding Frequency** — To specify how many thousand times per second the audio is sampled and recorded. A higher rate equals better sound quality but a larger file and more bandwidth needed to run it smoothly. Use the default 44.100 if viewers will run the movie from a CD, 22.050 for broadband, or 11.025 (but try 22.050) for a modem.

4. Click the Record button and start talking into the mike.

   Click the Pause button if you need to stop recording temporarily.

   Click the Stop button when you're through recording.

5. When you finish recording, click **OK**. You return to the Audio tab.

6. Click the Play button on the Audio tab to hear the clip.

7. Click **OK**.

Editing Voice Narration

Mimic isn't a full audio editor, but it does let you perform simple tasks like cutting or inserting silence and boosting or equalizing the volume of a clip. You can edit any audio clip, but you'll most likely use the editor for voice clips.

1. Double-click on the frame containing the audio clip to edit.

   The Frame Properties dialog box opens.

2. Select the Audio tab. You'll see the name of the audio file assigned to this frame in the Audio field.

3. Click the Edit button below the Audio field. The Sound Editor dialog box opens.

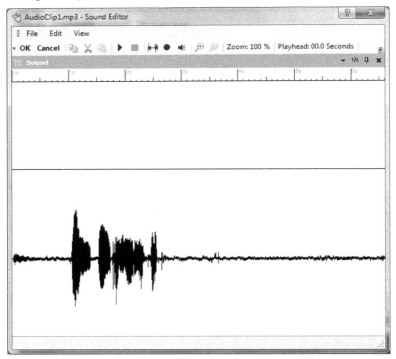

The toolbar offers the following options:

- Cut, Copy, Paste icons — Standard.

- Play and Stop icons — To play the clip or stop it.

- Record and Play icons.

- Zoom In/Zoom Out icons.

- Insert Silence icon  — To add silence. Clicking this icon opens the Insert Silence dialog box with four options.

- **Duration** – The duration of the silence.

- **Current selection** – Replaces any currently selected portion of the sound clip with silence.

- **Playhead position** – Inserts the silence at the play-head's current location in the clip, even if it's in the middle of a word. (A common but easily fixed error.)

- **Start.../End...** - At the start or end of the clip.

Click anywhere on the sound wave to see a vertical red line, the playhead.

To select part of a clip, such as a silent period to delete, click at the beginning of the period to select and drag left or right to highlight that part of the clip.

4. Make the desired changes.

5. When you finish, click **OK**.

6. Click **OK** to close the Frame Properties dialog box.

Adding Audio to Movies

You can add audio to a movie, usually as background. If a frame has a voice clip, the movie audio will continue to play in the background.

1. Select **File > Properties** or **Movie > Movie Properties**, or open the Frame Properties dialog box, select the Audio tab, and click the Movie button.

   In each case, the Movie Properties dialog box opens.

2. Select the Audio tab, shown below and make the appropriate settings.

Select the Enable Audio option at the top. Then select from these options:

- **Play, Pause** — To play or pause the selected audio file.

- **Edit** — To open the audio editor for an audio file that you recorded. This button is disabled for the audio files that ship with Mimic.

- **Pick Built-In...** — To use one of the audio files that ships with Mimic.

- **Pick From Movie Sound Library** — To select for re-use an audio clip that you already imported into the movie and that is now in the sound library. This holds down the movie size since you're re-using a clip that's already in the movie.

- **Import Into... Library** — To import an external audio clip in WAV or MP3 format into the movie.

- **Record a New Audio Clip** — Self-explanatory.

- **Loop Sound** — To play the file repeatedly until the movie ends. This eliminates the need to find a clip whose duration exactly matches that of the movie. Some of the clips that ship with Mimic offer looped versions, so you don't have to select this option if you use one of those clips.

   Tip – Select the Loop Sound option if the movie has frames with voice or the movie audio may stop after the last frame with voice

3. When you finish, click **OK**.

Using Frames From Other Mimic Movies

You may sometimes want to use frames from another movie in one you're creating. It's easy to do; open both movies simultaneously and copy and paste the desired frames from one movie to the other. However, before you do so, be sure both movies are the same size. If they use different screen sizes, you can still copy and paste the frames but the viewers will see inconsistent frame sizes in the finished movie.

Copying Frames From One Movie to Another

1. Open the movie that contains the frames to be copied and the movie into which to paste those frames.

2. Display the Frames pane for both movies.

3. Select the tab for the movie that contains the frames to be copied.

4. Right-click the desired frame(s) on the Frames pane and select **Copy Frame**.

5. Select the tab for the movie into which to paste the frames.

6. Right-click on the frame on the Frames pane after which to paste the copied frame(s). For example, to paste the copied frame(s) in position 3, click on frame 2.

   If you need a pasted frame in position 1, click on frame 1 and insert the frame, which puts it in position 2. Then use the Move Frame Up/down icons to move it into position 1.

Importing PowerPoint Slides

If you use PowerPoint, you can use it with Mimic to add flexibility to your work.

For example, you can import a PowerPoint presentation into Mimic and save it as a SWF to let users run it from a server rather than having to download and run it locally. This simplifies maintenance because you only have to update the movie on the server, without worrying about old copies on users' local PCs. Or you might import specific frames from a PowerPoint presentation into a Mimic movie for use as frames.

This section looks at both options – creating an entire movie based on a PowerPoint presentation and importing specific frames from a Power-Point presentation into a Mimic movie or collection.

Creating a New Movie from a PowerPoint Presentation

1. Start Mimic.

2. Select **File > New > Import PowerPoint**.

   The Import PowerPoint Wizard dialog box opens.

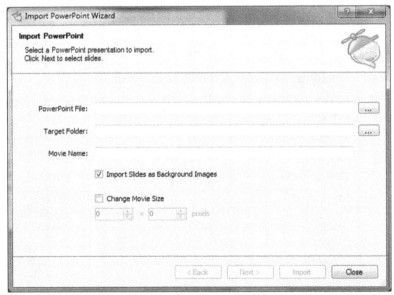

   Make the necessary entries in these fields and options:

- **PowerPoint File** – The file to import. Click the browse button to the right of the field to see the Open dialog box.

- **Target Folder** – The folder in which to store the file, if you want to store it in a different folder. If not, ignore this option.

- **Movie Name** – The name for the movie, if you want to use a different name than that of the PowerPoint file. If not, ignore this option.

- **Import... as Background...** – If the PowerPoint file contains screen objects like text boxes or images:

  - De-select this option to be able to edit the objects in Mimic. Select the option to merge the objects into the Mimic frame background. The objects will look just as they did in PowerPoint, but you won't be able to edit them in Mimic. You'll have to make any changes in PowerPoint and re-import the changed frames.

    Tip – The choice depends on whether you want to use PowerPoint as your prime development environment and use Mimic a "post-processor" or use Mimic as a total development environment.

- **Change... Size** – To make the imported movie the same size as the original PowerPoint frames. Select this option and specify the Height and Width if you want to use a different size but keep the aspect (height-to-width) ratio.

3. To import all the frames, click the Import button. To use a subset of the frames, or to check the frames, click the Next button. The second wizard screen opens and shows each frame's selection box, number, description (from the slide title), and an optional preview.

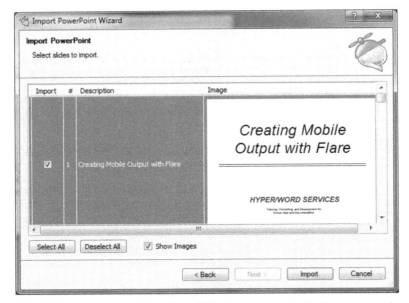

Use the Select All or Deselect All buttons to select all or none of the frames, or click on the import box for each frame that you want to import.

Deselect the Show Images option if you don't need to see the frame previews.

4. When you finish, click the Import button.

Mimic imports the frames and presents them as a new movie.

Importing PowerPoint Frames Into a Mimic Movie

1. Open the Mimic movie in which to insert the PowerPoint frames.

2. Select **View > Frames** OR click the Frames icon on the toolbar if you need to display the Frames pane.

3. Click on the frame in the Frames pane after which to insert the PowerPoint frames.

4. Select **Insert > PowerPoint Slide(s)** or click the Insert PowerPoint icon on the Frames pane toolbar.

The first screen of the Import PowerPoint Wizard opens.

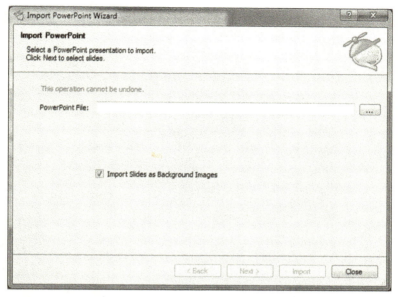

5. Click the browse button at the right of the PowerPoint File field to see the Open dialog box and select the file whose frames you want to import.

6. Deselect the Import... as Background... option if you want to be able to edit any PowerPoint frame objects, such as images, in Mimic. Select this option to make these objects part of the frame backgrounds and thus not editable in Mimic. (If you need to change any of these objects, you'll have to do so in PowerPoint and re-import the frames containing the changed objects.)

7. To import all the frames, click the Import button. To use a subset of the frames, or to check on the frames, click the Next button. The second wizard screen opens and shows each frame's selection box, number, description, and optional preview.

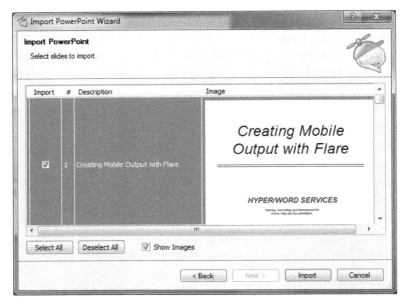

Use the Select All or Deselect All buttons to select all or none of the frames, or click on the import box for each frame that you want to import.

Deselect the Show Images option if you don't need to see the preview of the individual frames.

8. When you finish, click the Import button.

    Mimic imports the selected frames and inserts them after the frame you selected in the Frames pane.

Conditions

Imagine that you have to create one movie for two different audiences but show slightly different things for each audience.

For example, you may want to show one version of a callout for one audience and a different version of the callout for the other audience. Or, say that you have to create a movie to run on large-screen devices like laptops and small screen devices like iPhones. You decide that you want to show the callouts in the large-screen version but hide them in the small-screen version because the text is too small to read, and replace them with voiceovers. In each case, the answer seems simple – create one movie for each audience.

But this approach is inefficient since you have to maintain both movies. Better to create one movie that you can generate in different versions but only have to maintain in one place. That's what conditions let you do.

A condition is basically a category that you can apply to a frame or frame object. For example, you might create two categories called Audience_A and Audience_B. You then create two callouts on the same frame, one worded for audience A and one for B, and apply the appropriate category to each callout. To generate the output for audience A, you tell Mimic to exclude anything categorized as applying to audience B.

Or, in the large-screen/small-screen example, you define two categories and call them Large_Screen and Small_Screen. You then apply the Large_Screen category to the callout and the Small_Screen category to the voiceover. To generate the output for large-screen devices, you tell Mimic to exclude anything categorized as Small_Screen, and vice versa for the mobile output.

Tip – Categories can have unusual uses. For example, you might want to add author notes in each frame of a movie, but you can't since viewers would see them. But you could create a category called author_notes, add the notes in text boxes in each frame, apply the author_notes category to those text boxes, and tell Mimic to exclude anything flagged as author_notes from the output.

In each of these cases, the excluded material remains a part of the movie: it's just hidden on output.

In proper Mimic terminology, the categories are called conditions and the labels are conditional build tags, often referred to as "build tags."

The process is straightforward mechanically; the complexity lies in figuring out what you need to do. The steps:

1. Define what you want to accomplish with the conditions. Think ahead to what you might need to accomplish a year from now as your markets or strategies change.

2. Create the build tags.

3. Apply the build tags to frames and objects as needed.

4. Generate the output by including or excluding build tags as necessary and check to result to make sure it's what you need.

Note – You'll use conditions in three places – movies, collections, and "targets". Targets are the most logical place to use conditions because targets are used for single sourcing and conditions are one of the major features that enable single sourcing.

Creating Conditions In a Movie

A condition has a name, color tag, and optional comment. If you apply a condition to an object, Mimic adds the color tag to the object as a visual indication that the object has been conditionalized.

1. Select **Movie > Properties**.

2. Click on the Condition Tags tab.

3. Click in the first blank field in the Name column and type the name of the condition.

   Caution – Be sure all parties agree on the name before you start to apply it to frame objects. If you rename an applied condition, you'll break the connection and must re-apply the condition.

4. Click the pulldown in the Background field and select Pick Color. The Color Picker dialog box displays.

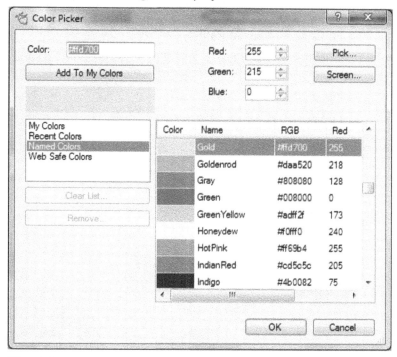

Tip – You can use this dialog box to pick recently used colors, named colors, or web-safe colors, or define a custom color by specifying red, green, and blue values in those fields or a hexa-decimal (base 16) value in the Color field. Your color will display in the preview box in the upper left corner. You can also use an existing color on the screen. To do so, click the Screen button, move the little picker window on top of an example of the color you want to use, and click. Here, we'll just discuss named colors

5. Click the Named Colors option, scroll down the color list, select the desired color for this condition, and click **OK**.

    Tip – Select strong colors that will stand out on the frame. If you need multiple conditions and may apply multiple conditions to the same object, be sure to select contrasting colors. In other words, don't select Antique White and Bisque for the same project.

6. Repeat steps 3, 4, and 5 if you need to define more conditions. When you finish, click **OK**.

Applying Conditions

Applying a condition is a simple matter of selecting the frame or frame object to be conditionalized, opening its properties dialog box, and selecting the desired condition(s).

1. Select the frame or frame object to be conditionalized and double-click it to open its properties dialog box.

2. Click on the Conditions tab.

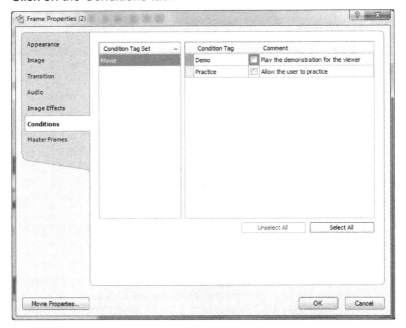

3. Click in the check box for each condition that you want to apply to the selected frame or object.

    Note that all you're doing here is assigning the condition to the frame or object. You're not processing; that's the next step.

    How can you tell if a condition has been applied to a frame or object?

    For a frame, view the Frames pane. If a frame has a condition applied to it, you'll see a little square of the same color as the condition to the left of the frame number. See frame 5 in the image below.

For an object, you'll see a little square of the same color as the condition on the object itself. See the upper left corner of the Nort text box in the image below.

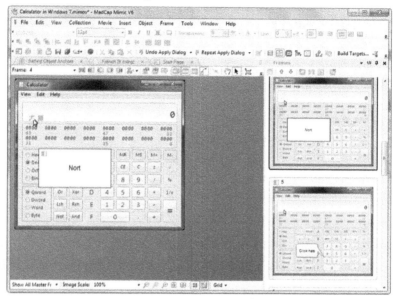

Generating Condition-Based Output

Once you apply conditions to your frames and objects, you can generate output that includes or excludes those conditions. You can do this for a movie or collection, but you're probably most likely to generate condition-based output for specific output targets.

1. To generate condition-based output for a movie, select **Movie > Movie Properties**, select the Conditions tab, select the desired conditions, and save the result.

   To generate condition-based output for a target, select the desired target or create a new target from the Movie Properties dialog box, go to the target's Conditions tab, select the desired conditions, and save the result.

2. To generate the movie, select **Movie > Build the Output Movie**

   or click the Build icon .

To generate the target(s), click the Build Targets button on the toolbar and select the targets to build from the list in the Build Targets dialog box.

Deleting Conditions

After a while, you may find that you're no longer using some conditions that you created previously. You don't have to delete unused conditions; you can simply ignore them.

However, the unused conditions clutter the Condition and Condition Tags tabs so you may want to delete them to clean up the interface.

1. Select **Movie > Properties**.

2. Click on the Condition Tags tab.

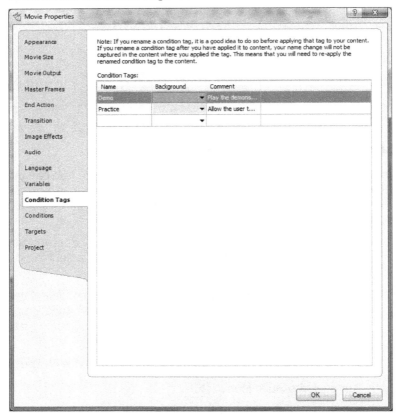

3. Click on the condition to be deleted so that the entire row is highlighted, then press the Delete key on your keyboard.

Using Conditions from a Flare Project

Mimic and Flare are highly integrated at a programmatic level. This lets you use conditions defined in a Flare project in a Mimic movie or collection, essentially integrating the two separate tools.

There are two ways in which you can use conditions from a Flare project in a Mimic movie or collection.

If you insert the movie or collection into a topic in a Flare project, the conditions are automatically integrated and will be available in the Conditions tab in a Mimic Properties dialog box.

If you do not insert the movie or collection in a Flare project, you can link them manually. This is a simple process that need only be done once. Here, for example, is the set of conditions in a Mimic movie project.

You decide to link the movie to a Flare project in order to share the conditions defined in that project. Follow these steps to do so:

1. Select **Movie > Properties**.

2. Click on the Project tab.

3. Click the browse button to the right of the Linked Project field and select the Flare project whose conditions you want to share.

4. Save the Mimic project.

The Conditions tab now shows these five conditions, the original two and three from the Flare project to which you linked.

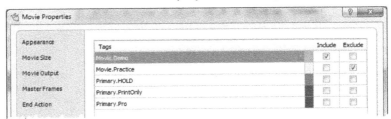

Work With Variables

It's not unusual to create a movie for a new product and refer to the product by name in callouts, only to have the name change before release. Or create a movie for a client to which you refer by name, only to have to modify the movie for a new client. In each case, you have to change all instances of the old name to the new one, a tedious and time-consuming job. Variables eliminate this.

A variable is a placeholder whose value you set. For example, you could create a variable called ProdName and set its value as Longhorn. To insert the name in text, you insert the variable ProdName; the viewer sees the value, Longhorn. If the product is renamed Vista, you don't have to find and replace each instance of Longhorn. Just change the variable value from Longhorn to Vista and the name changes everywhere.

There are three steps to using variables:

1. Create and define the variable.

2. Insert the variable. You can insert it in callouts, shapes (rectangles, circles, irregular shapes), and success, failure, and hint caption boxes.

3. Edit the variable to change its value, if necessary.

Types of Variables

You can create four types of variables:

- Movie – Apply to a single movie. You create them.

- Collection – Apply to all movies in a collection. You create them.

- System – Pre-defined by MadCap for system information like the date or a file name. You simply insert them.

- Project Link – Part of a Flare project linked to a Mimic movie. This means Flare and Mimic projects can share variables. See the section entitled Using Conditions from a Flare Project for information on how to connect a Mimic movie or collection to a Flare project in order to share variables as well as conditions.

Creating and Defining a Variable

In this section, you'll create a variable for a movie.

1. Open the movie in which you want to create the variable.

2. Select **Movie > Properties** OR click the Movie Properties icon on the Frame toolbar.

   The Movie Properties dialog box opens.

3. Select the Variables tab.

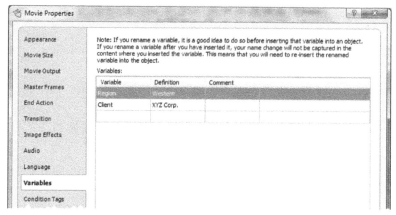

4. Type the variable's name in the Variable column.

Note – Do not change a variable's name after you insert it. Doing so breaks the connection to the variable and Mimic cannot update the values. You'll have to re-insert the variable everywhere.

5. Type the variable's value in the Definition column.

6. If necessary, type an optional comment in the Comment column.

7. Repeat the process on the next rows if you need to add more variables.

8. When you finish entering the variable(s), click **OK**.

Creating a collection variable is similar, but you do so using the Variables tab of the Collection Editor. To access it, open the collection and select **Collection > Properties**.

Inserting a Variable

After creating a variable, you can insert it in two ways:

- If you created a new object and are adding text, click on the object and start typing. An insertion box opens on top of the object. You can type and format the text, and click on the Insert a Variable icon in the upper left corner of the box. This opens the Variables dialog box where you can select the variable.

- Open the object's Properties dialog box, select the Rich Text tab, and add or change the variable.

Through An Object's Properties Dialog Box

1. Double-click on the object to which to add the variable.

   The object's Properties dialog box opens.

2. Select the Rich Text tab.

3. Position the pointer in the text where you want to insert the variable and click the Insert a Variable icon .

   The Variables dialog box opens, and lists the variables in the project.

4. Select the variable type (movie, system, etc.) in the left column, select the desired variable in the right column, and click **OK**.

   You return to the tab, which shows the variable in code form – [%=variable type.variable_name%] – [%=Movie.prodname%].

5. Click **OK**.

   You'll see the object in normal view with the variable in normal text mode.

Editing a Variable's Value

Editing the value is similar to creating a variable but you don't change the name. The change immediately appears everywhere.

1. Open the movie in which you want to edit the variable.

2. Select **Movie > Properties** OR click the Movie Properties icon on the Frame toolbar.

   The Movie Properties dialog box opens.

3. Select the Variables tab.

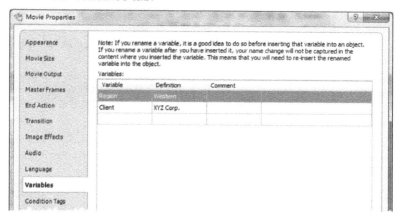

4. Type the new value in the Definition column.

5. If necessary, type an optional comment in the Comment column.

6. When you finish, click **OK**.

7. Select **Save All** to update the variable's value in all the insertion locations.

Editing a collection variable is similar to editing a movie variable, but you do so on the Variables tab of the Collection Editor. To access this editor, open the collection and select **Collection > Properties**.

Master Frames

There may be times when you want to insert specific features on multiple frames. For example, you might want to add navigation buttons labeled Previous and Next to let viewers back up or advance at their own pace. You could create the buttons and insert them on each slide but that's a tedious job, more so if you then decided to change a button's look or functionality and needed to replace it on each frame.

Master frames eliminate this problem. A master frame contains standard elements that you can over- or underlay on regular frame. For example, you could create a master frame that had a Previous and Next button and apply it to each regular frame in the movie. If you applied the master frame as an underlay, the navigation buttons would appear below the regular frames' contents. If you applied the master frame as an overlay, the buttons would appear on top of the regular frames' contents.

Or you might create a master frame containing a transparency of your company's logo and apply that master frame to each regular frame in order to get a watermark look on each frame.

Once you apply a master frame to regular frames, any change to the master frame is automatically applied to each frame to which you applied the master frame. For example, if you apply the master frame with the transparent logo watermark to the first ten frames in a movie, then learn that your company just adopted a new logo, you don't have to change it on each frame. Just change it once on the master frame and the change ripples across the ten frames automatically.

After creating a master frame, you can apply it to all frames in a movie or specific frames, and can remove it from specific frames. Note that master frames don't support image effects like zooming and blurring.

Tip – To use the master frames from one movie in another movie, open the first movie in Mimic, open its Master Frames pane, select and copy the desired master frame(s), open the second movie in Mimic, open its Master Frames pane, and paste the master frame(s).

Tip – An alternative to the previous approach is to add the master frame to a frame library, then open the frame library in the other movie in Mimic, and copy the frame from the frame library to the master frame of the second movie.

Creating Master Frames

Creating a master frame is similar to creating regular frames.

1. Open the movie in which you want to create the master frame.

2. Select **View > Master Frame > Master Frames** to open the Master Frames pane.

   You can also select View > Master Frame and:

- Show All... - To show all master frames applied to the movie.

- Show Top...- To show all top master frames applied to the movie.

- Show Bottom... - To show all bottom master frames applied to the movie.

- Hide... - To not show any of the master frames applied to the movie.

3. Insert a new frame using the appropriate Frames menu command below:

   To create the master frame from scratch, click on any frame in the Frames pane and select **Insert > Blank Frame**.

   To copy an existing frame and make it the basis for the master frame, click on that frame in the Frames pane and select **Frame > Duplicate Frame**.

   In either case, you'll wind up with a new frame.

4. Add the common elements to the frame, using whatever Mimic features or Frame Properties dialog box tabs are necessary.

   For example, here's a frame created for use as a master frame, with the photo of the telescope as the common element added in the upper left corner, but the frame itself not yet turned into a master frame. You know that because the frame is not yet on the Master Frames pane and because the frame's background on the Frame pane is grey.

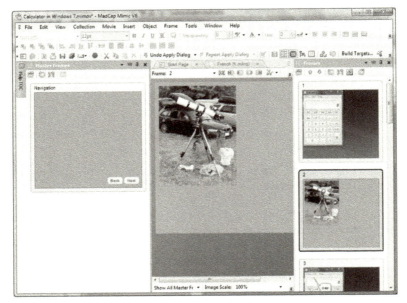

5. When you finish setting up the frame elements and are ready to turn it into a master frame, select **Frame > Add Frames to Master Frames**.

    The frame now appears in the list on the Master Frames pane, as shown below. Note also that the frame's background on the Frame pane is now blue, indicating a master frame.

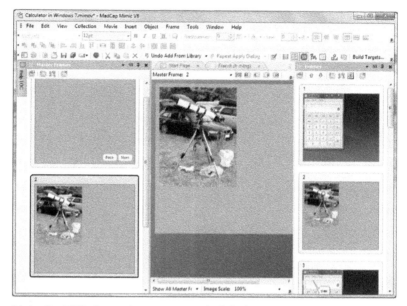

Note that Mimic assigns a numeric label to a new master frame, such as 2 for the example above. This label is accurate but not very useful since the number won't mean anything to you when you have to select a master frame from a list of master frames. It's good practice to change the label to a textual description.

To assign a text label to a master frame:

3. Double-click the master frame on the Master Frames pane. The frame opens in the Frame pane with the blue background, and the Master Frame Properties dialog box open to the Appearance tab.

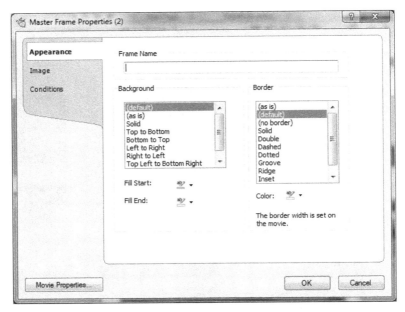

The Appearance tab offers these options:

- **Frame Name** — To add a text name for the master frame. You can't use spaces between words in multi-word names. Use underscores.

- **Background** — To set the background color as solid or as a color gradient in different directions.

- **Fill Start/Fill End** — To set the starting and ending colors if you set a gradient for the background.

- **Border** — To set the master frame's border style.

- **Color** – To set the master frame's border color.

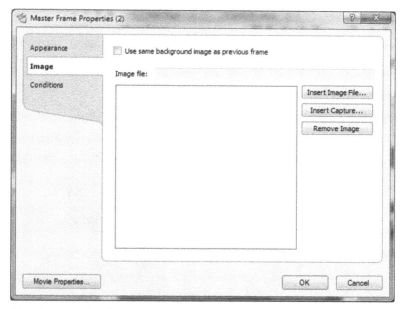

The Image tab offers these options:

- **Use Same Background Image as Previous Frame** — To replace any image in this frame with the one from the previous frame.

- **Insert Image ...** — To insert an existing image in the master frame.

- **Insert Capture...** — To capture a new image and insert it in the master frame.

- **Remove Image ...** — To remove the bitmap from the master frame.

The Conditions tab is the same as the Conditions tab discussed in the Callouts section in the Basic Frame Annotation chapter.

2. Add the text label in the Appearance tab and make any other necessary settings.

Applying a Master Frame

After creating a master frame, you can apply it to individual frames or to all the frames in a movie.

To Individual Frames

This approach is good if you only need to apply a master frame to a few specific frames in a movie. However, it's inefficient if you need to apply the master frame to a large proportion of the frames. In that case, you may find it more efficient to apply the master frame to all the frames in the movie and then remove it from the small number of specific frames to which it doesn't apply. It's simply a matter of balancing your efforts.

1. Right-click on the frame to which to assign the master frame in the Frames list OR the Frame pane and select Pick Master Frames.

   In either case, the Pick Master Frames dialog box opens.

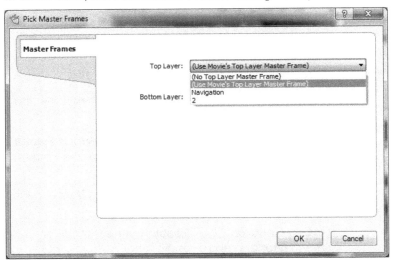

3. Open the Bottom Layer or Top Layer field pulldown, depending on whether you want to apply the master frame as an underlay or an overlay, select the desired master frame, and click **OK**.

Tip – Display the Master Frames pane before opening the Pick Master Frames dialog box in order to have a visual reference as to your choices.

Tip – Whether or not you display the Master Frames pane first, it's easier to select a master frame if you give it a descriptive, text label in place of the default numeric label.

To All Frames At Once

This approach is good if you need to apply the master frame to all but a few specific frames in a movie. However, it's inefficient if you need to apply the master frame to a few frames. In that case, you may find it more efficient to apply the master frame to the specific individual frames.

1. Select **Movie > Properties**.

   The Movie Properties dialog box opens.

2. Select the Master Frames tab.

3. Open the Bottom Layer or Top Layer field pulldown, depending on whether you want to apply the master frame as an underlay or an overlay, select the desired master frame, and click **OK**.

4. Select each individual frame in the Frames pane from which you want to remove the master frame, right-click, and select Remove Master Frames to remove the master frame from that frame.

Editing a Master Frame

Editing a master frame is similar to editing a regular frame, except for how you access the master frame. You can access it in two ways:

- From the Master Frames pane.

- From a regular frame to which you applied the master frame.

From the Master Frames Pane

This approach is good if you're making a planned change to the master frame.

1. Select **View > Master Frame > Master Frames** to open the Master Frames pane if necessary.

2. Click on the desired master frame to open it in the Frame pane and edit it like any other frame.

From a Regular Frame

This approach is good for spur-of-the-moment changes if you're editing a regular frame and see something in a master frame that needs changing.

1. Right-click on the frame in the Frames list and select Edit Bottom Layer Master Frame, or right-click on the frame in the Frame

pane and select Edit Top or Bottom Layer Master Frame.

In either case, the master frame displays in the Frame pane.

2. Make the desired changes.

Deleting a Master Frame

1. Select **View > Master Frame > Master Frames** to open the Master Frames pane if necessary.

2. Right-click on the master frame to delete and select **Remove Frame**.

Adding a Master Frame to a Frame Library

1. Select **View > Master Frame > Master Frames** to open the Master Frames pane if necessary.

2. Right-click on the desired master frame and select **Add Frame to Library**.

Frame Libraries

There may be times when you want to use identical frame(s) in multiple movies. For example, you might want to use the same copyrights frame in all your movies. You could create that frame from scratch for each movie, but that's inefficient and it's easy to introduce small differences each time. Plus you'd have to maintain each instance of the frame.

A frame libraries fixes this. A frame library contains predefined frames for use in as many movies as you need. Just create the frame to be re-used, store it in the library, and select it as needed. Simple...

Flare ships with one frame library containing predefined frames for objects and tasks like progress indicators, navigation, and branding. You can use these frames, customizing them for your specific needs, and/or add frames to the frame library. You can also create new libraries if you want to categorize your frames, delete existing frame libraries, and add a frame from a library to a list of master frames.

Using a Frame From a Frame Library

This is the basic use of a frame library.

1. Select **View > Frame Libraries**.

    The Frame Libraries pane opens.

2. If you have multiple libraries, click the Library pulldown on the Frame Libraries pane and select the desired library.

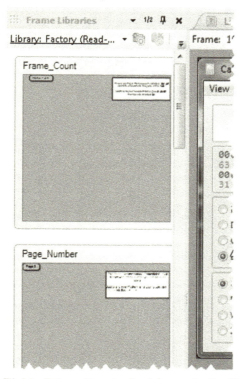

3. Right-click on the desired frame in the library pane and select Add Frame to Movie. Mimic adds the frame in the last position in the movie.

4. Move the frame to the desired position in the movie.

Adding a Frame to a Frame Library

You can add your own custom frames to libraries that you create.

Note – You cannot add frames to the Factory (Read-Only) library that comes with Mimic.

1. Select **View > Frame Libraries**.

   The Frame Libraries pane opens.

2. If you have multiple libraries, click the Library pulldown on the Frame Libraries pane and select the one to which to add the frame.

3. Right-click on the desired frame in the Frames pane or the Frame pane and select **Add Frame to Library**. Mimic adds the frame to the library.

Deleting a Frame From a Frame Library

You can delete your own, unused frames from libraries that you created. You don't have to delete unused frames, but too many unused frames will clutter up a library. If you have frames that you're not using but are afraid to delete, you can create a new library, name it something like "Probably Unused...", and cut and paste the unused frames from whatever library they're in to the new one.

Note – You cannot delete the pre-defined frames from the Factory (Read-Only) library that comes with Mimic.

1. Select **View > Frame Libraries**.

   The Frame Libraries pane opens.

2. If you have multiple libraries, click the Library pulldown on the Frame Libraries pane and select the one from which to delete the frame.

3. Right-click on the desired frame and select Remove Frame.

Creating a New Frame Library

You don't need to create new frame libraries if you just want to use the frames in the library that comes with Mimic. But you do need to create new frame libraries if you want to add your own frames to a library, and can create multiple libraries if you want to categorize your own frames.

1. Select **View > Frame Libraries**.

   The Frame Libraries pane opens.

2. Click the Create a New Library icon on the Frame Libraries pane.

    The New Library dialog box opens.

3. Type the name and click **OK**.

    You return to the Frame Libraries pane on that library and can now start adding frames to it.

Deleting a Frame Library

You can delete a frame library if you're not using the frames on it or just want to consolidate several libraries into one so as to unclutter the Mimic interface.

1. Select **View > Frame Libraries**.

    The Frame Libraries pane opens.

2. Click the Library pulldown on the Frame Libraries pane and select the library that you want to delete.

3. Click the Delete This Library icon on the Frame Libraries pane.

    A dialog box asks for verification.

4. Click **Yes** to delete the library.

    You return to the Frame Libraries pane at the last library you used.

Making a Frame In a Library a Master Frame

You may decide that you want to designate a library frame as a master frame.

1. Select **View > Frame Libraries**.

    The Frame Libraries pane opens.

2. Click the Library pulldown on the Frame Libraries pane and select the library that contains the frame that you want to turn into a master frame.

3. Right-click on the frame to turn into a master frame and select **Add Frame to Master Frames**.

The Master Frames pane opens and displays the frame, which also appears in the Frame pane in case you want to edit it.

You can now use the frame like any other master frame.

Palettes

With so many options available for Mimic's annotation objects, it's time-consuming to recreate the same annotation object on multiple frames and hard to do consistently. Instead, you can create "palettes", groups of objects that you can reuse without having to define them from scratch each time. It's simple; you create the rough object and add it to a palette. Finally, select it from the palette for reuse in different frames or movies. You still have to add any unique content – text in a callout, for example, but you're already defined the basic object.

Mimic comes with several palettes containing predefined arrows, loops, bubbles, and rectangles to let you start adding objects immediately. It also comes with an additional palette, called MyPalette, to which you can add your own objects. If you want to categorize your objects, you can easily create additional palettes – callouts, for highlight boxes, and so on. You can also delete a palette that you're no longer using.

Palettes also support consistency. Palette files are stored in a My Documents\My Palettes folder with a .capal extension, so you can create a palette and send its file to all the developers.

Displaying the Palettes Window

To display the Palettes window, select **View > Palettes** or click the Open the Palettes Window icon ⬚.

Adding An Object to a Palette

Add the object to the MyPalette palette that displays when you open the Palettes window. To add the object to another palette, create and/or display that palette by following the directions in later sections.

1. Create the object, or open the frame that contains the object if the object already exists.

2. Select **View > Palettes** OR click the Open the Palettes Window icon ⬚ on the standard toolbar.

The Palettes window displays.

3. Right-click on the object to add to the palette and select Add to Palette. The object displays on the palette.

Adding an Object To a Frame From a Palette

Adding an object from a palette is a simple double-click or click and drag.

1. Select **View > Palettes** OR click the Open the Palettes Window icon ![icon] on the standard toolbar.

   The Palettes window displays.

2. If you created extra palettes and want to use an object from one of them, click the Palettes pulldown on the Palettes window toolbar and select the desired palette.

3. Double-click on the desired object or drag the object from the palette to the frame.

4. Double-click on the object to open its Properties dialog box and make any necessary changes.

Adding a Palette

You can add new palettes if you want to categorize your objects rather than putting them all on MyPalettes, or if MyPalettes is getting too full.

1. Select **View > Palettes** OR click the Open the Palettes Window icon ⬚ on the standard toolbar.

   The Palettes window displays.

2. Click the Create a New Palette icon ⬚ on the Palettes window toolbar.

   The New Palette dialog box opens.

3. Type the new palette's name and click **OK**.

   You return to the main screen, with your new palette selected.

4. Add objects to the new palette as necessary. You can copy an object on one palette and paste it to another palette.

Note – You cannot undo an action that spans multiple palettes, such as cutting an object from palette A, pasting it into B, then deciding to restore it to palette A.

Deleting a Palette

You can delete a palette that you no longer use. Copy objects that you want to another palette before deleting the old palette.

1. Select **View > Palettes** OR click the Open the Palettes Window icon ⬚ on the standard toolbar.

   The Palettes window displays.

2. Click the Palettes pulldown on the Palettes window tool-bar and select the desired palette.

3. Click the Delete This Palette icon ⬚ on the Palettes window toolbar.

4. A message asks for confirmation.

5. Click **Yes**.

   You return to the Palettes window, and the palette is no longer available.

Tip – To share a palette between multiple authors, search for and copy the CAPAL file for the desired palette. The CAPAL files should be in the C:/Users/Owner/Documents/My Palettes folder on your PC.

Link Browser Window

When you work on a movie one frame at a time, it's hard to see the big picture of all the frames and their inter-connections, or between movies in a collection. The Link Browser window provides that picture, showing all the frames in a movie and the links between them, or the movies in a collection. You can then select any frame to look at its properties, modify the links, or delete the frame.

The Link Browser window toolbar has two options.

Icon	Name	Description
	Edit frame properties	Opens the Frame Properties dialog box for the selected frame. (You can also right-click on the desired frame and select Frame Properties.)
	Remove selected frame	Deletes the selected frame.

1. Open the desired movie.

2. Select **View > Link Browser** OR click the Link Browser Window icon on the standard toolbar.

   The Link Browser window displays.

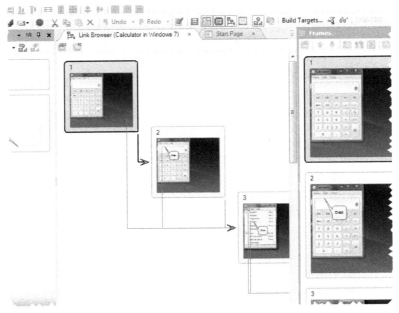

3. Click on any frame in the window to highlight it and boldface its link arrow.

4. To display the Frame Properties dialog box for the selected frame, click the Edit Frame Properties icon OR right-click on the frame and select Frame Properties.

   To display an individual frame, double-click on the frame in the Link Browser window.

   To delete the selected frame, click the Remove Selected Frame icon .

   Use the horizontal and vertical scroll bars to see all your frames.

5. When you finish, close the window.

Templates

How do you make your movies or collections look consistent if you have to create multiple movies or collection or you're one of several authors? You *can* define standard settings and require their use when creating a new movie or collection, but this is slow and prone to being overlooked. Instead, use a template.

A template is a file of the same type as one you want to create. For example, if you want to create a group of movies with some standardized settings, you can create a movie that contains the settings and save it as a template. When you want to create a new movie, you base it on that template. Open the template, save it with the name of the new movie, and add that movie's specific content. The template inserts the standard features, saving time and reducing inconsistencies. And saving the copy of the template with the name of the movie creates the movie *and* saves the template for use for the next movie. Simple…

However, if you work like this, sooner or later you'll add a new movie's content to the template but forget to save it with the name of the new movie, thus overwriting the template.

The solution is to integrate the templates directly into Mimic's interface. This way, when you create a new movie or collection or import a skin, Mimic will ask what template to use. You can pick it from a list, without worrying about template names or other housekeeping chore. Mimic does that for you. Note that Mimic comes with pre-defined "factory templates" which may meet your needs. If so, you can ignore the rest of this discussion.

After you create the templates and store them in specific subfolders, you can create a new collection or movie or import a skin. A dialog box will ask you to select the template; the Templates Folder list will default to listing the factory templates but you can select My Templates and get a list of the templates you created earlier. After selecting a template, you can then create the collection or movie or import the skin, but using the settings from *your* template.

Where to Store Templates

Create a folder called My Templates under the My Documents folder (or Documents folder in Windows 7). Then, if you're creating a:

- Collection template – Create a subfolder called Mimic Projects in the My Templates folder and paste the collection template folder there.

- Movie template – Create a subfolder called Mimic Movies in the My Templates folder and paste the movie templates there.

- Skin template – Create a subfolder called Mimic Skins in the My Templates folder and paste the skin templates there.

The next time you create a new collection or blank movie or import a skin you can select the My Templates folder in the dialog box and select from the templates that you added.

What the Templates Should Contain

You can use any collection, movie, or skin as a template. However, if you do, with a movie for example, the template will contain material that's peculiar to the original movie and may have nothing to do with the other movies that you want to create. It may be more efficient to create minimalist movies that contain only the common features that you want to use in your template.

Creating a Movie Template

The principles of template creation are similar no matter what type you're creating, so this section just describes one type – a movie.

To use an existing movie as a template:

1. Create the movie to use as the template for new blank movies.
2. Open Windows Explorer.
3. Go to the My Documents folder.
4. Create a new folder and name it **My Templates**.
5. Click on the My Templates folder and create a new subfolder called Mimic Movies.
6. Go to the folder containing the movie to be used as a template and copy that movie's mimovf file.
7. Go to the Mimic Movies folder and paste the mimovf file.
8. Return to Mimic.

To create a blank movie from a template:

1. Select **Movie > New Movie > Create Blank Movie.**

   The Add New Movie dialog box opens.
2. Click on My Templates in the Template Folders list box. You'll see your templates in the Templates list box on the right.
3. Click on the desired template in the Templates list box.

4. Fill out the remaining fields, then click Add and finish creating the new project.

Mimic "Collections"

So far, we've focused on creating movies. This section describes collections and how they differ from movies. Consider this example.

You create two movies, a demonstration and a simulation, about a topic and want to define the movies such that when viewers reach the last frame of the demonstration, they see the question "Are you ready to try it yourself?" and two buttons labeled "Yes" and "No, show me once more."

Clicking "No" takes them to the first frame of the demonstration where they can watch it again. You can set up this button using the GoToFirst option in the Button Action tab of the Button Properties dialog box. Clicking "Yes" takes them to the first frame of the new movie. You can set up this button using the Open or OpenWithDefault option in the Button Action tab of the Button Properties dialog box. So a standard movie is fine; there's no need to create a Mimic collection.

The problem with this approach is that it uses an absolute path to the target – i.e. the target movie must be where you specified in the link code. If it isn't, the link won't work - movie file location is crucial. You also have to be sure you generated the target movie. So movie management is also crucial. A Mimic "collection" is a simpler option.

A Mimic "collection" is a set of movies treated as a group. By making the movies part of a group, Mimic can keep track of their locations, which makes linking between them easier and more predictable.

You can work with collections in two ways:

- Create the new collection, then create movies from within it.
- Create the new collection, then import existing movies into it.

The steps in this process are similar to those for creating a regular movie – create, annotate, output, and publish. What's new is the creation of the collection itself and Mimic's collection-related features.

To create a collection:

1. Select **File > New > Movie Collection**.

   The first screen of the Start New Collection Wizard displays.

2. In the Project Name field, type the name for the collection.

3. Click the Browse button and select or create a folder to contain the collection, then click Next to go to the next wizard screen.

4. To use a language other than US English for the spell checker or a Flash skin, select that language here. Otherwise, click Next to go to the next wizard screen.

5. Select the desired template.

6. Click **Finish**.

The Collection Editor pane opens.

- The Sections tab lets you:

  - Create new movies within the collection, or import existing movies or PowerPoint presentations into the collection.

  - Rename a movie in the collection.

  - Change the title of a movie in the collection.

  - Open a movie in the collection if you need to make sure it's the right one.

  - Delete a movie from the collection.

  - Change a movie's position in the sequence.

- The Options tab lets you control the output settings. It's very similar to the Movie Output tab on the Movie Properties pane except for the skin.

- The Skin tab lets you edit the skin, but a collection doesn't offer the embedded skin option.

- The Language tab lets you set the language for the spell checker and for any foreign language skin if you're creating Flash output.

- The Variables tab lets you define a variable for the collection.

- The Condition Tags tab lets you define new conditions or change an existing condition's marker color.

- The Conditions tab lets you specify whether to apply a condition and whether to apply it as an include or exclude.

- The Targets tab lets you define or edit an output target's settings – title, output format, skin, variables, or conditions.

- The Project Link tab lets you link to a Flare project.

7. Select **Save All**.

After creating a collection, you can create movies within it or import movies into it.

To add movies to a collection:

1. Open the collection and click the Sections tab in the Collection Editor.

2. Click the appropriate option on the Collection Editor toolbar:

   - The Create Blank... option opens the Add New Movie dialog box where you can create a new movie normally.

   - The Import Mimic Movie option opens the Import Movie dialog box, with two fields:

     - **Source File** – The desired movie's mimov file. Click the browse button to the right of the field and select the desired mimov file.

     - **File Name** – The selected movie's title. Mimic automatic-ally enters this. You can change it if necessary.

       Note – Any conditions in the movie are not imported.

3. Specify the Source File field entry.

   That movie's file name displays in the File Name field.

4. Click the Import button.

    You return to the Collection Editor's Sections tab and the movie opens.

5. Repeat the process to import additional movies into the collection.

6. Select **Save All**.

    After adding movies to a collection, you can define the output settings and create the finished product.

To define the output settings and create the output:

1. Open the collection whose output settings you want to define and click the Options tab in the Collection Editor.

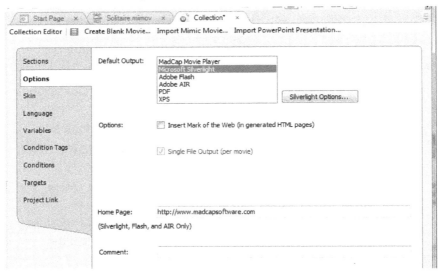

This tab is similar to the Movie Output tab. To recap the options:

- **Default Output** – The desired output format.

- **Silverlight Options** – To specify how many frames to load before the movie begins to run. The more frames loaded the less the risk of "stutter" but the longer the movie takes to begin.

- **...Mark of the Web** – For Flash output. Hides the "blocked content" warning that displays if you open an HTML file on your local PC. You don't need this option if your movie will run on a server.

- **Single File Output** – For MadCap Movie Player output. To create one file that contains the entire movie for ease of distribution. Deselect this option to create multiple output files, which means you have to distribute more files but the individual files are small and load faster.

- **Home Page** – For Silverlight, Flash, or AIR output. To specify the URL for a home page that viewers can access by clicking a Home icon on the tool-bar. You define the Home icon through the Skin Editor.

- **Comment** – For any developer comments.

2. Select the desired output format and options.

3. Select **Save All**.

4. Select **Collection > Build**

—OR—

Click the Build the Active Movie/Collection icon on the standard toolbar.

The Build Progress dialog box opens.

5. When the build ends, click the View Output button to run the movie, or click Yes if a message asks if you want to view the output.

The movie displays in the appropriate player for the output format you selected.

6. Close the player and return to Mimic.

Integration with Flare

Mimic is part of MadCap's MadPak suite, so it integrates with Flare. You can insert a Mimic movie into a Flare help topic. From a Flare topic, select **Insert > Multimedia > Flash Movie or Mimic Movie** from the Flare menu.

Index

A

About Box tab

Skin editor, 109

About icon

Modify on toolbar, 112

Accordion labels, 16

Accordion list color, 15

Action tab

Bubble properties, 60

Rectangle properties, 150

Add callouts, 44

ADDIE methodology

Analyze, 29

Design, 30

Develop, 33

Evaluate, 35

Implement, 35

Align images, 87

Animation Effects tab

Bubble properties, 59

Button properties, 143

Appearance tab

Button properties, 142

Frame properties, 80

Input Box properties, 155

Master Frame properties, 190

Movie properties, 101

Rectangle properties, 149

Appearance tab:, 53

Arrow tab

Arrow properties, 73

Arrows, 68

Create, 70

Arrows tab

Polygon properties, 72

Audio

Add to frames, 162

Add to movies, 168

Add to objects, 161

Loop clip, 83

Overview, 159

Supported formats, 83

Tips, 159

Tips for voice narration, 159

Voice narration

Edit, 166

Record, 164

Audio Input Source, 44

Audio tab

Button properties, 161

Frame properties, 82, 163

Movie properties, 168

Auto-hide Windows, 25

Automatic frame advance, disable, 147

B

Back up a movie, 40